Camping Cookbook

The ultimate guide to preparing healthy and delicious recipes while camping

By

THOMAS MENZIE

Table of Contents

Introduction

Camping can signify various things nowadays, for example, pop-up tents or campers and casual tents. These are good ways of emerging in the woods; there is nothing as genuine as camping in an outdated way and laying down for a night or two in a sleeping bag and tent. By far, camping is one of the ways of enjoying beautiful landscapes. It is a perfect way to take a break and detach from the everyday world and your busy schedule. You will also not have reliable electricity and the internet, allowing you to take a quick detox, destress, and observe the beauty of nature.

One will investigate the fire, intrigued by the gurgling flames, watching as the flickering bits of ash rise upward and vanish into the dark sky. There's nothing like deep sleep to the squeaking cricket sounds and then getting up to a sound of wind chimes and a fresh breeze in the morning. Falling asleep overnight in a camp in the middle of the woods may seem ridiculous for those that have never been camping yet. But for those who love mother nature and adventures would enjoy every bit of it.

Better still, if you invest in the right equipment, camping is reasonably inexpensive. Camping only includes a tent, a sleeping bag, and maybe a small campsite fee, while many holidays come with costly hotel and activity charges. Camping is an affordable choice to consider if you are seeking a quick family escape on a budget. You should save expenses and go on field trips to the areas of your desire as you grow up, instead of taking expensive holidays abroad. While it might not seem as thrilling as a visit to Disney World, there is a great experience to be had in the natural surroundings for adults and children. This is because of such camping trips that enthusiasm and love for nature can be created, something anyone can prosper from.

In this book, you will get to know all the essential things required for camping and how you can make your camping trip memorable with delicious recipes and amazing food.

Chapter 1: Camp Organization Regarding Kitchen

In this section, we will briefly discuss the camp organization regarding the kitchen.

1.1 What to Bring for Camping?

Your relaxation and desire to love your trip to the fullest degree will significantly influence how you prepare for camping. You can have a horrible time if you get the wrong gear.

You will find the things needed for camping below.

1. Solar charger for phones

After all, in the natural surroundings, you will not find many power outlets. Using the sun's energy, a solar adapter with a USB connection may charge your camera, phone, light, or other gadgets. This waterproof device hooks onto the backpack of yours so that while hiking, you could let it capture sunlight.

2. Paracord Rescue Bracelet

Anytime you go into the woods, this agile little device is important. It has an emergency bell, compass, small knife, and fire starter built-in in contrast to the long 12-foot paracord. It's also customizable and very affordable for any wrist size. Outside without one, I may never go hiking or camping.

3. Packing cubes

You will want a collection of quality packing boxes like these if you want to be able to quickly find stuff in your tent, backpack, or car. Instead of going through it all, you brought to see if there is one clean denim, take out the cube where you packed your denim. This is a game-changer in camping.

4. Cooling Towel for Chilly Pad

When trying to remain cool in the blistering heat, a chilly pad is a lifesaver. All you must do is soak the towel, strain out the extra water, and then feel temperature around your body, face, and shoulders 30 degrees cooler. You will never go on camping without it after you try it. It lasts 3 to 4 hours, and then all you need to do is soak it again, and its magic that will continue to work. And it costs virtually nothing.

5. Sleeping bag

If you are in a season-appropriate, waterproof sleeping bag, sleeping under the sky and star would be much more pleasant. Attempting to camp lacking one which will give you enough warmth is often downright risky. This one is sturdy, lightweight, and simple to clean- check the temperature requirements and intend to remain comfortable and safe.

6. Tent

It is necessary to choose the right tent. A decent tent is fully weather-resistant and simple to make. The size and style of tent you select may depend on the size and space needed for your group, but this is a model that is durable and very well-ventilated. It is also one of the camps on the market with the most inexpensive standard, and it will last for several years.

7. Windproof Umbrella for Travel

Without the necessary rain cover, nothing is worse than being trapped in a rainstorm when camping. But if you carry a quality weather-resistant travel umbrella, then no matter what the weather ends up being like, you will be sure to be protected. One must weigh less than one pound, should be super lightweight, and come with a replacement guarantee.

8. Solar lantern

This is particularly important when banning fire when the stars and the moon are the only sources that light your path. A solar lantern is perfect because no battery or energy source needs to be modified. My favorite is a collapsible one, easy to carry, and bright, plus it should be light enough to take with you and place for inside lighting in your tent.

9. Camping Parachute

There is nothing like resting in a hammock underneath a big shady tree at the end of a long walk. This hammock should be compact, lightweight, quick-drying, and easy to clean. All you must do is identify the perfect trees, and in no time, you will be set up.

10. Blister Balm for feet

You'll be on your feet all the time when you camp and will probably do a little hiking that brings extra stress on your heels. Bring this incredible blister balm to stop the agony of blistered feet, and you're not going to have a problem. By preventing the extra friction which triggers blisters, it drifts on easily and lasts a whole day.

11. Filtered bottle of water

When camping, it's so necessary to carry a reusable, good-quality, distilled water bottle. Without thinking about how safe the source is, you should refill it at your camping area's water spigots because it eliminates 99.99 percent of the waterborne microbes, which would otherwise make you ill. You can also securely gather water from a river or stream right away.

12. Quality Cooler

Choosing what to cook and how to protect your food from dropping dead is the trickiest aspect of camping. Bring burgers, hot dogs, or something else you would like to barbecue for dinner if you bring a camping stove (or a fireplace on-site). Some nice variations are bacon and yogurt or eggs with granola for breakfast. Ensure you have spatulas and metal tongs with you and store perishable food in an ice-filled quality cooler.

13. Gas stove

Bringing a gas stove is a handy way of cooking meals, particularly if your campground doesn't have a barbecue. One is super cheap, easy to manage, lightweight, and made of good-quality materials by Coleman.

14. Kit for first aid

On a camping trip, a lot could be done wrong. With a very well-stocked first aid supplies, be alert for splinters, blisters, bruises, and other far worse blunders. Carry it in your backpack so that in case of an emergency, you can whip it out.

15. Deodorant wipes

You will not be able to shower as often as you do at home when camping, and you will probably get sweaty and stinky. Bring a couple of these wipes instead of stressing whether your campmates would detect your odor. Take them out when you are in your tent or restroom, and you will be stink-free and revived with one quick clean.

16. Bear Spray

Black bears inhabit many of the best camping spots and national parks in North America. Hence, it is a no-brainer to bring bear spray when camping. You will also want to carry your food with bear-proof containers so that a bear doesn't attempt to break into your vehicle or tent at night. Besides, reports show that bear spray could also protect you from mountain lions roaming most of the same bear habitat.

17. Hydration daypack

Staying organized with a durable daypack that won't hurt your back is vital. If you'd rather be minimalist and only bring the water you need, this one by Camelbak is incredibly well built for day hiking. It's super lightweight and carries 50 oz, which is enough for a few hours to keep you hydrated.

1.2 Which Pots or Pans Are Suitable for Camping?

Perhaps basic cookware is required by backpackers, who make short journeys or desire simple, hardly any-fuss menus, maybe as little as a spork and a cup. Typically, campers, bigger groups, and prolonged trips need more sections. This segment gives you a rundown of your choices for outdoor kitchenware.

Individual pieces or cook sets?

A full collection of cookware or cookware goods can be purchased bit by bit.

Cooking sets are collections designed to assemble the pots, pans, and lids. Some cooking sets contain extras that nest inside the containers, such as plates, mugs, or cups. Individual parts allow you to build your collection pretty much the way you desire it. If you're trying to save weight for traveling and backpacking, this approach might not be suitable. It's a good way, though, to incorporate flexibility into your set of cookware.

Material Choices for Cookware

1. With Aluminum

Pros: Inexpensive, lightweight, and a perfect heat conductor. Nice without scorching for bubbling foods.

Cons: starts to break down progressively when subjected to acidic foods.

2. Hard aluminum

Pros: This material form is oxidized and is long-lasting and prevents abrasion and scratches.

Cons: Zero.

3. Steel

Pros: Thicker, more resistant to scratching than aluminum.

Cons: Heavier than aluminum does not conduct heat as evenly (can cause food to be scorched by hot spots).

4. Titanium

Pros: Extremely lightweight, without compromising strength, it's your lightest choice. Highly resistant to corrosion, easily heats up and works efficiently without full heat. Cons: More costly than other alternatives. It conducts less uniform heat than stainless steel. Take care to prevent it from overheating.

5. Cast Iron

Pros: For cooking or baking, it is ideal and tough.

Cons: Heavy, not really for backpacking applications. Proper care is taken.

6. Non-stick coatings (accessible on certain metal cookware)

Pros: Keep the breeze clean.

Cons: Less resilient than normal metal surfaces. Many could be scratched by utensils made of metal.

7. Plastic

Pros: Affordable, Lightweight, non-abrasive. Great for utensils and airtight food containers.

Cons: not quite as durable or resistant to heat as metal. Many plastics may pick up food odors or flavors and hold them.

Safety issues for cookware

1. Aluminum: Some individuals wonder whether it's unsafe to use aluminum cookware. There are no health issues associated with using aluminum pans, pots, or skillets, based on studies from the drug and food administration, National Institutes of Health, and the Alzheimer's Society of London. The Alzheimer's Society states: "There is no definitive medical or empirical evidence of a correlation between aluminum and Alzheimer's disease." though not a health issue, it is not advised to cook cauliflower or leafy greens or in aluminum cookware because it can affect the taste and appearance.

2. Non-stick coatings: If seriously overheated, cookware equipped with a food-grade fluoropolymer will emit toxic fumes. Inhaling these gases in humans may induce flu-like symptoms, and pet birds have been likely to be killed by them. While cooking with non-stick cookware, use caution (for example, not to use it when broiling food) or try using uncoated alternatives instead.

3. BPA: A synthetic compound of significant concern for older cookware is bisphenol A (BPA). All cookware products offered by REI are free from BPA.

Other Considerations for Cookware

1. Pot size: roughly the largest pot must be 1 pint per camper or backpacker in your party.

2. The number of pots depends on how many backpackers are in your group and the sort of cooking you expect to do. If you're planning to cook dehydrated food for two backpackers, one pot is enough. Extra pans and pots are required for more complex meals and bigger groups.

3. Lids: Lids decrease cooking time, preserve fuel, and lower splatter. For each pot, some cookware features a lid, while some have a single lid, which can be used on many pots of various sizes. Some lids can also act as plates, that can make your load lighter.

4. Pot grippers or lifters: Ensure that you have a way to safely catch your pans and pots. For all the pans, most cooking sets contain one gripper. Remember to pack it up for you.

5. The advantages: Some cook sets come complete with utensils, plates, mugs, and even towels. If you are starting from zero, this is useful or may be unnecessary if you're not.

Utensils

Although car campers can use conventional kitchen utensils, many backpackers trying to save weight and space have tended to gravitate to the spork. This convenient spoon/fork combination offers great versatility. A little knife on the side of an outer tine is also included in some sporks.

Don't forget to carry spoons, spatulas, and whisks for measurement, as needed.

Kitchen gadgets from camp

With these facilities onboard, campers do not have to "rough it":

1. French press: It is a coffee maker (also available for campers).

2. Extension forks: for hot dogs or marshmallows to roast.

3. Cooking Iron: for grilled sandwiches.

4. Dutch oven: A slow cooker for stews, meats, and more.

5. Popcorn popper: at the campfire, always a success.

6. Also, carry spice pots, squeeze bottles, and items for washing.

1.3 How to Make A Bonfire?

The campfire is a cherished and essential outdoor ritual for many, a luminous, kinetic, dreamlike natural phenomenon that has served as the centerpiece of backwoods gatherings for centuries.

The main steps for creating a good campfire are discussed in this section and fire safety tips, whether you are car camping or backpacking.

1. Find or Build a Fire Ring

Campgrounds: Build fires in specified fire rings, fireplaces, or grills only. Most of these built campsites have some version. Using a fire ring will demonstrate your effect and keep the fire confined.

Often check with the operator of the campground to make sure that fires are allowed. Extreme dry periods in some areas can cause campfires, even in campgrounds, to be prohibited.

Suppose you are camping in an undeveloped area, check-in detail with the land management agency (U.S. Forest Service, Land Management Bureau, etc.). It can require a campfire permit.

Before starting the fire, assess the location. Keep your fire tiny or miss it entirely if the site has low-hanging branches or is bushy. Fly-away flames could quickly spark a wildfire in dry conditions.

Backcountry: If one has been left behind, choose an existing fire ring in backcountry areas where wildfires are allowed. Make a new one only in emergency circumstances and dismantle it when you are finished if the situation permits. If one still exists, before you leave, wipe it out.

Clear all the explosive stuff out of your fire pit. Ideally, gravel, sand, or mineral soil (often found on gravel bars or in streambeds) should be the foundation of your flames. Intensive heat will sterilize healthy soil, so conscientiously choose your place.

A mound-fire is an alternative to a fire pit. Create a circular, flat base of mineral soil (light-colored, sandy, no fertile dirt) approximately 6-8 inches high using a sanitation trowel. Using this as your firebase. Build this framework on a flat rock, preferably. When you're done, you can quickly scatter the mound.

2. Gathering Firewood

You will need three fuel forms to burn a good fire: kindling, Tinder, and firewood.

Small twigs, dried leaves, forest duff, or needles are used in Tinder.

Kindling is made up of small sticks, generally about less than one inch.

Firewood is any bigger piece of wood that will keep the fire burning into the night for a long time.

Campgrounds: Use local firewood only. Nearby shops also hold firewood, and campground hosts often sell for sale packages of kindling or firewood.

If you're going more than 50 miles south, do not carry wood with you. Despite the distance you drive, campgrounds can also prohibit carrying your firewood, to discourage problematic insects from being introduced into the forest.

For information and guidance, contact the campground or a nearby ranger bureau in advance.

Backcountry: Pick only down timber far from your site if you search for firewood. Never destroy live trees or split branches from dead or standing trees. Snags and Dead branches are used by wildlife and birds.

Do not collect or gather the burnt pieces thicker than that of an adult's wrist. This is because it is seldom permitted to burn thick pieces of wood entirely and are commonly left behind as unsightly, blackened scraps.

Note to follow the principles of Leaving No Trace while collecting wood.

3. Build your Campfire

Cone: Begin with a small kindling cone around some handfuls of Tinder, loosely stacked in the center of the ring of fire. Once the fire is high and the temperature rises, you can introduce larger logs a few at a time as needed.

Log Cabin: To shape your building base, put two bigger firewood pieces parallel to one another and with some space in between. Then turn 90 degrees and add two marginally smaller pieces to create a square at the top and perpendicular. Within the square, place plenty of Tinder. Keep adding a few more firewood pieces across the perimeter, with each layer becoming a little smaller. Finish over the top with a sheet of Tinder and kindling. Consider leaving space among logs so that there is plenty of oxygen available for the flames.

Upside down (pyramid): Begin side-by-side on the bottom layer with three or four of your largest logs. Turn 90 degrees and then connect to the top of the second layer of relatively smaller logs. Continue alternating a few more layers in this manner, becoming smaller as you go. Place the Tinder and your kindling on top.

4. Lighting the Campfire

With a lighter or match, illuminate the Tinder. The Tinder can help capture the flame by using a fire starter that is built to ignite quickly. (Be sure to bring waterproof Firestarter and matches. Fire-making materials are expected one of the Ten Essentials.)

Blow gently at the firebase after lighting the Tinder to provide oxygen, which will greatly boost the flame's strength and further ignite the wood. Shift the embers to the middle as the fire burns, to burn them full. You should preferably limit them to white ash,

5. Extinguish the campfire

Often review their guidelines with traditional land managers and obey their measures if they have them. Generally, though, by dumping water on it (be cautious not to stand where the steam will scald you), swirling the ashes, and adding more water, you can extinguish the fire. Repeat as frequently as required. Before you leave the spot, the Ashes must be cool to the touch. Be completely certain that before you leave, the fire and its members are cold.

Notice that the practice of extinguishing a fire with soil or sand is problematic because it can protect coals, which can later be exposed, igniting a wildfire.

Never leave an unattended campfire.

6. The Campfire Clean up

Burn trash goods only if they're fully consumed and converted to ash by flames. Do not try to burn cardboard, containers, or plastic. If you burn something that is not completely consumed, when the fire is out, gather the remains and then either pack it out or drop it in a waste bin.

Pack out any garbage contained in your pet while you're in the backcountry. Within your ring, remove any charcoal pieces remaining, take them away from your location, smash the chunks, then disperse the remains and dust over a large area. Destroy any structure that you may have constructed.

1.4 Ways to Cook on A Campsite.

Over the years, outdoor explorers came up with many ways to use a campfire for cooking meals. Some are far more complex than others, of course. For example, mostly camping trips would probably not need you to make a roasting spit (unless you feel a little busy). Follow up as we explain some of the easiest, most efficient strategies of camp cooking.

Using direct heat is the most primary method of campfire cooking. There are 2 ways to do this. Firstly, the trick of old boy scouts is to individually roll food items in a foil of aluminum and put

them in heated coals. This needs regular testing, but for the foods that need high heat, it is very successful. Secondly, the strategy is merely to put a grill on an open flame and grill the food in the backyard as you would. The warmth from this origin is not direct, so cooking will probably take a bit longer.

You'll need the pans and pots listed above in the supply list for soups, stews, and pasta. Just build a fire to cook them, let it decrease to the heated coals, and put the pan or pot over them. The trick to this technique is to control hot coal volume and concentration, as warmth can become erratic quickly. The great news is that cooking in camp is just as simple as using a kitchen stove once you're done with it.

Some tips

1. Measure the ingredients ahead of time for every meal and store them in ziplocked bags. Mark should bag correspondingly.

2. In advance, prepare chili, stews, soups, etc. Freeze and cool down. Reheat it for a fast meal.

3. Do not skip the aluminum foil, which is highly durable. At camp, there are several benefits to it.

4. For gas canisters, be very cautious. Always keep yourself awake. Hold it in a well-ventilated place outside. By placing liquid soap on all links, check for leakage. When not being used, turn it off.

5. Freeze the meat before placing it in a cooler. It keeps most foods cool and can last longer.

6. Cover pots during outdoor cooking. Food will be cooked faster. It also helps in keeping the food safe from dirt and insects.

7. Put soap which is in liquid form on the outside of the pans and pots before placing over the flames for ease of cleaning and to protect against fire damage and smoke.

8. Ice in block form would last longer as compared to cubed ice.

9. In waterproof bags or containers, all products in the cooler must be packaged.

10. Keep food hidden, or sway above floor level, to prevent unwelcome encounters from animals.

11. To prevent food from sticking, add oil to the camp grill.

12. Frozen juice cans hold to keep the other food items cooled.

13. For fast meals, use convenient foods.

14. Use cooking equipment, which is fireproof. Keep the handles free from flames and intense heat.

15. To keep matches and matchbox dry, dip them in wax and erase the tip of the light and match when needed. Keep your matchbox in a waterproof jar as well.

16. For food storage such as sauces, soap, chili, etc., use Ziplock bags. Defrost the bag, then drop it in the cooler. It keeps the food cool.

17. Use paraffin wax, in melted form, in and around the leaky region to repair a coolant leak.

18. Put a bucket of hot water on the flame as you feed so that when you will be free, it will be prepared for cleanup.

19. Keep it in a pocket and swing from a tree to keep the soap clean at your camping spot.

20. Pita bread loads better and remains in better condition than normal style bread when camping.

21. Between these meals, carry energy-enhancing snacks like granola bars, beef jerky, dried fruits, etc.

22. To make hamburgers uniformly throughout, place a hole about the size of your finger in the center of your hamburger. The hole will vanish during grilling, but the mid will be fried like the same way as that of the sides.

23. Load soda bottles 2-liters or gallon milk jugs with juice or water and defrost. These keep the cooler cool and supply a cold liquor.

24. Wipe a solution of baking soda and water to clear odors from the cooler.

25. Use a different beverage cooler so that the cooler with food doesn't open too much.

26. Refill your ice regularly. To prevent food from spoiling and poisoning, keep the food cool.

27. Add powdered sugar in a little amount to the container to prevent the marshmallows from clinging together.

28. Boil the eggs in a bottling ring while preparing egg sandwiches using English bagels or muffins.

29. If you add a recipe with so much salt, add a potato which is peeled in the plate and finish cooking. Excess salt will be consumed by potato.

30. Use your leftover meat and vegetables on the last day of camping to make breakfast omelets. In omelets, you may use virtually any ingredient so that you would not have to carry the leftovers with you home then.

31. Ingredients pre-chopped at home, such as onions, tomatoes, etc. Store in containers for Ziplock. For rapid meal preparation, select the pre-cooked meat and freeze it.

32. Store food goods in distinct Ziplock containers. It's simple to pack. Resealable. It can be used when empty, for garbage cans.

33. Try "squeeze" a margarine. When in the bush, this squeezed bottle is very much simpler and smoother to use. It is perfect for colder temperatures as well. Simply put that bottle in a container of hot water for a minute if it becomes too hard.

34. Cook over or on charcoal. Coals, without smoke, have much more consistent heat. Avoid undercooked or burned food.

35. Use the pots as mixing bowls to conserve space while packing for the camp kitchen.

36. For fast cooking and quick cleanup, heavy foil of aluminum takes up less space and are perfect for mixing meats and vegetables.

37. Roast the chicken without a sauce while barbecuing chicken, unless it is half cooked and then covered with sauce. The sauce will not burn on the chicken, and it will make your meal tastier.

38. Use a charcoal chimney to have your pieces of charcoal prepared faster.

39. For sauces, salad dressings, and oils, disposable bottles of water make perfect dispensers.

40. Add some drops of dishwashing liquid or enough water to cover the bottom of the pan and bring it to a boil to quickly remove burnt food from your pan or skillet.

41. Use a big ancient pot of coffee to warm up water for cleaning the dishes or cooking.

42. Use a work glove made of leather or suede as a hot pad.

Different styles of fire starters that are home-made.

1. Fund in airtight sealed containers or bags if you are really into outdoor camping. Bacteria do not grow fast without air, and cold foods have seemed to keep getting better. In airtight containers, arrange servings for individuals so that you only access what you desire. For iced goods, individual parts defrost more rapidly than larger ones. Using them for your trash because the containers are reusable. They are smaller than cans as well. Eventually, the containers are thicker than most storage containers and can reduce the food's scent if not remove it. **2.** Use 2-4 wide coffee cans full of water and wrapped as grill holders with heavy foils of aluminum. Water gets hot for washing

or cleanup when your meal is cooked. To keep residue from other products, store them in their plastic bags. Fold the plastic bags for storage, along with dishcloth or soap, etc.

1.5 How to Set Up and Use A Gas Stove?

It is possible to use camping gas stoves wherever you need to cook food and without a kitchen. Perhaps just in a campground where fires are banned, you might be tailgating. Modern models of camping stoves are lightweight and compact and provide simple installation. When you are out in the forest, learning how to use these stoves safely and efficiently would help you.

Stove Setup

1. Remove all the bits from the bag that came with the stove. Generally, camping stoves come in multiple separate parts that need to be linked. Removing all the pieces from the backpack offers you a pleasant rundown of the items you have and work.

2. Within the bag will be a sheet of paper or card with a list of the things to include with the stove. To have double verification that you have everything, you can use this list. A connected hose, bottle of gas, the stove should be there, and depending on what type of stove you get, there might be a few other small things.

3. Do not assemble the burner or stove if things are missing, as it may be hazardous.

4. Using the gas line, attach the gas canister to the stovetop. This is the primary link for you to be capable of cooking that needs to be created. By twisting, the gas line can attach to the stove, but depending on the type of stove you have, it might be different.

5. A metal container is a canister, and the gas line is typically composed of hose-like material.

6. Be cautious not to twist so hard. If the gas line is already successfully attached, you can most certainly hear a clicking sound.

7. To search for leaks, splash soapy water on gas connector sites. Wait to observe if any bubbles emerge at the attachment points until you have sprayed the water on them. This indicates a leaky link if bubbles occur, and you should try to attach the gas line to the burner and canister again.

8. You are likely to move on when there are no bubbles present.

9. The use of any standard dishwashing soap mixed in a spray bottle with water works well here.

10. The gas should also be set to 'off' here as you search if any leaks are coming from locations that should not be there.

11. Use a paper towel, pat the attachment points dry. There is a chance of the residual liquid stopping you from burning the stove if you keep these points wet.

12. Use a towel or any other combination of materials if you do not have a paper towel.

13. To put the stove on, find a flat surface. The stove must be flat while you are cooking, or there is a danger that it will tip over. Not only is this risky, but it is also potentially inefficient and unbelievably inconvenient.

14. Build a flat surface if you need to dig some of the ground out and stack it up to build a flat field.

15. The surface on which you have the stove should be as stable as possible. Stop any terrain with the ability to move as you cook on it.

Operating the stove

1. Split the arms across the burner so that they are equally spaced apart. These weapons form the core support where your pan will sit. The arms are clustered together when the burner is packed tight. By lifting them and moving them around the burner, spread them out.

2. The stove would not get something placed on it without these arms expanding into the correct location, since it would only be an open flame.

3. It's common to have four arms, but your burner may only have 3.

4. Use the priming pump of the canister, pump the gas 15-20 times. This causes pressure buildup from the liquid fuel, which is used to turn it from a liquid to a gas form. Pump unless you can feel the pump's strong resistance (about 15-20 pumps).

5. The priming pump is typically a black pump that can come out either vertically or horizontally at the gas canister's peak.

6. This could require fewer or more pumps, and you must look at what the supplier of your stove recommends.

7. Open the gas line to pull out about 0.5 tsp (0.083 fl oz) of petrol. The fuel will go out to a small catchment area around which the flame develops. To heat the gas line and provide a place where the liquid is transformed into gas to burn effectively, this little bit of fuel is required.

8. It does not have to be precisely 0.5 tsp (0.083 fl oz). To burn, you only need a small quantity of fuel.

9. Turn the control knob that's connected to the stove to open the gas line. It appears like a paperclip on the knob.

10. Flash the fuel with a camp lighter or match in the catchment area. This method is called "priming" the fuel, and by transforming the liquid fuel in the pipe into a gas, it effectively does the spark's role on a standard stove.

11. Use a long lighter or match to light up the fuel and when you do this, be cautious not to burn your palm. It will be burned down very quickly when you strike the flame on the liquid.

12. Before moving into the next stage, let this fuel almost completely burn out.

13. Using the adjuster, change the fire to the size you need. The stove is now fully illuminated and prepared to be used as a standard stove. Therefore, opening the fuel adjuster gives you a bigger flame, and the flame is diminished by shutting it off.

14. Usually, the adjuster is attached to the stove, which looks like a paperclip connected to the stove.

15. Be vigilant not to turn the fire down too low, or you would have to go through this preparation process again to restart the stove.

16. Get your windbreak sheet set up. This is a thin sheet made of aluminum that you can place around the stove to prevent the flame from being disturbed by the wind. Most camping burners come with one, and if you are cooking in windy weather, they are a big help.

17. Set the windbreak sheet in a circle to work most efficiently.

18. Put some rocks around the side of the break to keep it in place if the wind is especially strong.

19. Cook down. Your stove is ready for cooking now. To change how big the flame is, use the fuel adjuster. Ensure that you let the parts cool a bit once you are done before carrying them away as they're hot.

20. It can take a little longer to cook on a small gas stove as the flame you are using is not quite as hot as home burners, so be careful.

21. Most types of pans and pots work fine on these stoves, so you can even roll food in a foil made of tin and cook it over the flame.

1.6 What Is the Best Food for Every Occasion and Season?

It is one of the joys of camping to make a meal using only a couple of ingredients you have brought along if the ingredients you have selected are light and versatile. There are ten simple 'base' ingredients around which to create smart campsite dining dishes, whether you are having a camping stove or carrying pre-made ingredients

1. Halloumi

As it retains its shape and has a high melting point, this firm sheep's milk cheese handles very well in a cool pocket. The durable quality of halloumi indicates it can be cooked to a somewhat meat-like texture in chunks or slices. Fry or griddle it, and skewer it to roast on a campfire or offer in wraps with some salad greens and dressing.

2. Flatbreads

Flatbreads fold up into a tidy, versatile stack, ideal for fitting into a hamper or rucksack, unlike an adequate loaf. Either eaten cold smudged with hummus or baked with typical tomato toppings and cheese, they can be converted into a pizza. Or go and zip back some melty quesadillas or use them for a zingy wrap of chicken and lemon.

3. Chickpeas

Canned chickpeas that are ready-prepared are much more convenient than that of the dried variety that needs soaking. For a versatile side dish, pour them straight into a bowl and dress them with vinegar, oil, and herbs. Alternatively, add them to a pot or use them as the salad base.

4. Chorizo

Find yourself a cured Spanish sausage of decent quality, nestle it into your backpack. As it is ready-cured, chorizo is the ideal camping sausage, so it can be eaten as a snack or sliced, crisped up in an omelet to also be served for breakfast with smoky beans and eggs, or mixed in a hash with potatoes.

5. Eggs

They may have to be perched and carried with relative care atop your clothing, but eggs are perfect camping fodder. Omelets can take all sorts of fillings (it's a nice way to use your chorizo). Eggy bread is also a classic breakfast at the campsite.

6. Sardines

All the tinned fish is perfect for camping, but they sound more like a whole meal since sardines typically come in chunky fillets. serve breakfast on sourdough bread, lunch with zesty lemon

and canned chickpeas, and supper with fennel, spaghetti, and broccoli (not always on the same day.)

7. Poches of rice

As among the most versatile grains, the basis for so many great meals are rice.

They are small and compact even if already cooked and can go from camping stoves to plastics plates in a few minutes. It can be added to a bean salad, used as a burrito filling, turn them into a hot and spicy curried pilaf, or make Chinese style egg fried rice.

8. Pasta

Pasta is a much-loved comfort ingredient, regardless of shape or size, which governs in a league of its own. Usually, slender spaghetti is better for saving space, but fusilli and penne are more palatable once they have gone cold. Instead of bacon, make a carbonara with sausage, put a fresh pesto pasta salad together or melt creamy cheese into a sauce of mushrooms.

9. Tinned fruits

It's always a case of mixing rather than cooking when it applies to camp desserts. Tinned fruit can be combined into an instant salad but melt some caramel to drizzle over tinned pears if you'd like to add a special touch, and sprinkle with hazelnuts. Sweet, shiny fresh peaches with cream are delicious too.

10. Ready-made dishes

And we are not talking about lasagne in the oven. One of the easiest ways to cook for your campers is to make just one-pot dish at homes that can be served off-site. Pre-made meatballs or ragu can be served and spilled over spaghetti in tomato sauce, chili can be eaten with campfire-baked potatoes, and couscous can be eaten with stew. Only please ensure it has been properly cooled and store in a cold setting.

Chapter 2: Breakfast Recipes

Breakfast is one of the essential things while camping. A healthy breakfast keeps you fresh and capable of hiking and more adventures.

1. Teriyaki Beef Jerky

Prep Time: 10 minutes, Cook Time: 4 hours, Serving 10

Calories: 188kcal

Ingredients

- 1 lb. Eye of round or top round

- ¼ cup Soy sauce

- 2 tbsp Mirin

- 2 tbsp Brown sugar

- 1 tbsp Piece of fresh ginger (1-inch), minced/pre-grated

- 2 cloves garlic, minced

- 1 tsp Salt

- ¼ tsp Prague powder

- 1 tsp Sesame seeds

Directions

1. Round the beef into bits that are 1⁄8-1⁄4-inch-wide, eliminating as much noticeable fat as

2. necessary. Put and set aside in a wide zip-top bag.

3. In a shallow cup, blend the brown sugar, soy sauce, mirin, minced ginger & garlic, cinnamon, and Prague powder until the sugar dissolves. Pour the meat into the zip-top container, taking care to ensure the meat is covered uniformly. Put the marinade in the fridge for 12-24 hours.

4. Place the strips on the dehydrator trays after the meat has cooked. Sprinkle the seeds with sesame. Dehydrate for 4-6 hours at 160F, before the meat has dried. If you bend a piece and it splits, the universal rule of thumb is that it's over-if you bend a piece and it falls; it's been fried too much longer.

5. Separate from the dehydrator and set it aside in a bag or Tupperware to cool fully prior to sealing.

6. Jerky marinated with Instacure or Prague powder can last at room temperature in a sealed bag for a few weeks. Jerky, marinated without any remedy, can stay in your fridge for two weeks.

2. Peanut Butter & Jelly Granola Bars

Prep Time: 5 minutes, Cook Time: 28 minutes, Serving 6

Calories: 270kcal

Ingredients

- 1 ½ cup Rolled oats
- ½ cup Jam
- ¼ cup Peanut butter
- 2 tbsp Brown sugar
- 1 tbsp Coconut oil
- ¼ tsp Salt
- ¼ cup Peanuts chopped

Directions

1. Preheat the oven to 350 with parchment paper or foil, cover a 9X5 loaf sheet.

2. Spread the oats for 10 minutes on a baking sheet and fry in the oven, adjusting at the 5-minute mark to confirm that they are uniformly toasted. Take it out of the oven and set it aside.

3. In a shallow saucepan, heat the jelly, peanut butter, sugar, oil, and salt. Simmer over medium heat for about 3 minutes until it thickens slightly, stirring continuously. Dump the toasted oats and swirl to thoroughly coat them in the pot.

4. Move the mixture in an even layer to the lined loaf tub. In the mixture, press the sliced peanuts onto the end.

5. Bake the bars until golden brown for 15 minutes. Take it out of the oven and leave to cool. Remove the rods from the pan and use a small knife to carve them into bars.

Notes

9x5 loaf pan Parchment paper or foil Baking sheet Small saucepan Mixing bowl Sharp knife Measuring cups & spoons (Equipment needed)

3. Bulls Eye Toast

Prep Time: 2 minutes, Cook Time: 10 minutes, Serving 1

Calories: 262kcal

Equipment

- Camp Stove

Ingredients

- 1 thick slice bread

- 1 tbsp Butter/oil

- 1 large Egg

- 2 tbsp Scallions

- Salt & pepper

Directions

1. Cut a ~2″ hole in the middle of the bread or pinch it. fire up the skillet and smear on one side of the bread 1/2 tablespoon of the butter (if the butter is soft, this works better)

2. Place the toast, butter side down, in the skillet. Directly break the egg through the cavity in the bread.

3. If the whites are set, and the bread is browned, apply the leftover butter to the top of the bread (this works well if it's smooth), and then use a spatula to turn the toast gently and cook the other side. Cook, once they are to your taste for the yolks. To try, top with salt & pepper.

4. Grilled Halloumi Breakfast Sandwich

Prep Time: 5 minutes, Cook Time: 15 minutes, Serving 1

Calories: 651kcal

Equipment

- Camp Stove

Ingredients

- 1 large Hawaiian sweet roll, (use the sandwich buns if you can find them)

- 1 tbsp Butter/oil

- 2 oz- sliced Halloumi cheese

- 1 egg

- 3 tbsp Mayo (3 tablespoons)

- 1 tbsp Sriracha

- 1 scallion (sliced or julienned)

- Salt + pepper

Directions

1. Or in your pan or over a fire, toast the sandwich buns. Only put aside.

2. Over medium-high melt, melt half the butter or oil in your skillet. Add the cheese until melted. Fry in spots on either side until golden brown, between 3-4 minutes on each side. Only put aside. If you've got one going, this move may also be achieved on a barbecue. Miss the butter/oil in that case and put the cheese directly on the grill.

3. Over a medium melt, heat the remaining butter or oil. Crack the egg into the pan until it is melted. Totally optional step: You can use a fork to blend the yolk a little until the whites begin to set so that it gets spread a little across the egg, so in every bite, there will be yolk. Cook the egg for about 4 minutes or until it's cooked to the perfect amount of doneness.

4. Prep the hot mayo when the egg is boiling. Mix the mayo and the Sriracha together in a small bowl (or in a measuring cup).

5. To assemble, on each cut surface of the buns, spread the spicy mayo in Layer to sample with the egg, scallions, grilled halloumi, and salt & pepper.

5. Sweet & Spicy Breakfast Skillet

Prep Time: 5 minutes, Cook Time: 20 min, Serving 2

Calories: 251kcal

Ingredients

- 1 tbsp Olive oil

- 1 large Sweet potato (cut in 1/2-inch cubes)

- 2 Poblano peppers removed stems, cut in 1/2-inch pieces

- ½ tsp Salt

- 2 C Kale (chopped)

- 3 Minced Cloves garlic

- 2 Eggs

Directions

1. Heat olive oil over med-high heat in a skillet. Stir in the tomatoes, sweet potato and half tsp. Salt until the oil starts to shimmer. Cook for 7 to 10 minutes, before softening starts, stirring regularly so that the vegetables are cooked uniformly. Add the kale and garlic and simmer until

the kale is soft for an additional 3-5 minutes.

2. Shift them over to one side of the skillet until the vegetables are finished.

3. If needed, add further oil, then into the empty half of the skillet, beat the eggs. Cook until you like the eggs; we want them fried in the center but always runny.

4. Season with pepper and salt, break between two bowls and enjoy.

6. Asparagus Pancetta Skillet Hash

Prep Time: 5 minutes, Cook Time: 20 minutes, Total Time: 25 minutes, 2 servings

Calories: 380kcal

Ingredients

- 1 tbsp Oil (1 tablespoon)

- 1 med & peeled Potato (if desired cut into 1/4-inch dice)

- 1 bunch Asparagus (-cut into 1-inch pieces)

- 4 oz- Pancetta (diced)

- 1 clove garlic, minced

- 1/4 tsp Sea salt (plus more to taste)

- 2 Eggs

Directions

1. Prepare the potatoes: Firstly, heat the oil on your stovetop over medium heat. Add the potatoes in an even layer until the oil is hot. Cook for about 8 minutes, rotating regularly until the potatoes begin to turn translucent so that both sides have a chance to shine.

2. Cook the asparagus & pancetta: Add to your skillet the asparagus, pancetta, garlic, and sea salt. For an additional 8-10 minutes, continue cooking until the pancetta is fried, and the asparagus is cooked through and tender.

3. **Fry the eggs:** To build a well in the middle of the skillet, shift the hash to the left. Crack the eggs into the well and cook them to the perfect doneness (to produce a strong white and a runny yolk, we cover the skillet and boil for 3 minutes).

4. **Serve:** Serve directly, either in a large skillet or split into two pans.

Notes

This can easily be made vegetarian by omitting the pancetta. (make it vegetarian)

7. Breakfast Scramble with Sun-Dried Peppers and Spinach

Prep Time: 5 minutes, Cook Time: 10 minutes, Serving 2

Calories: 313kcal

Ingredients

- ¾ cups Ova Easy
- 1/2 cup Sun-dried peppers (chopped)
- ½ cup Dehydrated spinach
- ½ tsp Garlic powder
- ½ tsp Salt
- ½ tsp Ground black pepper
- 1 tbsp olive oil/1 packet olive oil
- 1 ¼ cup-10 oz Water

Directions

1. **At home:** In a zip lock or little jar, apply the Ova Easy and spices (pepper, garlic powder, and salt), spinach, and peppers (large enough to add water at camp

   and blend).

2. **At camp:** To the baggie of eggs & vegetables, add 1 1/4 cup (10 oz) water. When fully mixed, blend with a fork or spoon and no lumps of egg left. Put aside so that the spinach has time, about three minutes, to rehydrate.

3. Heat the oil in a boiling pot or pan over low heat. Add the peppers and spinach and egg mixture.   Using a spoon, mix the eggs as they cook, taking care not to scorch the eggs until in the pot there is no liquid egg left if the pan is small. Yeah. Dig deep.

8. Pönnukökur - Icelandic Pancakes with Skyr

Prep Time: 5 minutes, Cook Time: 15 minutes, Serving 14

Calories: 108kcal

Ingredients

- 5 Eggs

- ¼ cups Flour

- 1 tsp Salt

- 2 ½ cups Milk

- Butter, ghee, or coconut oil

- 2 packages Icelandic Provisions skyr

- Strawberries, blueberries, or fruit of choice (cut into bite-sized pieces)

Directions

1. In a cup, beat together the chickens, milk, and salt until frothy. The flour is applied steadily, whisking until a fluffy batter emerges. Only put back.

2. Over medium cook, cook a non-stick or well-seasoned cast-iron skillet. Add a little butter to cover the bottom of the pan until the pan is warmed. Load in only enough flour to cover the pan (approximately 1/3 cup if a 10' skillet is used) and lift up the sheet, tilting it towards both sides so that the flour covers the bottom of the sheet in a thin layer evenly.

3. Using a spatula or knife to gently turn the pancake until the pancake has baked and the top is golden brown (30 seconds to a minute). Cook for an estimated 30 seconds to brown the other rim, then shift the pancake out of the pan and onto a tray.

4. Repeat with the remaining batter, utilizing more butter, if needed.

5. To eat, on one half of the pancake, scatter a piling spoonful of Icelandic Provisions skyr and sprinkle with some fresh berries. Cover the pancake over the filling in half and then, again, in half. Appreciate.

Notes

Adapted from The Nordic Cookbook by Magnus Nilsson

9. Cream & Strawberry Quinoa Porridge

Prep Time: 25 minutes, Cook Time: 10 minutes, Serving 2

Calories: 630kcal

Equipment

- Dehydrator
- Dehydrator Tray Liner
- Backpacking Pot
- Backpacking Stove

Ingredients

- 2 cups Water
- 1/8 tsp Sea salt
- 1 cup Quinoa
- 3 tbsp Maple syrup
- 1 tsp Vanilla extract
- 1 tsp Ground cinnamon
- ½ lb. Strawberries
- ¼ cup Coconut flakes
- ¼ cup Coconut milk powder

Directions

(At Home)

1. Rinse under running water with quinoa. Carry the water, quinoa and salt to a boil,

    cover, and simmer for 20-25 minutes. A few minutes, stir. As required, add additional water. Stir in the maple syrup, vanilla extract, and ground cinnamon remove from the sun.

2. Meanwhile, split the strawberries thinly and place them on a dehydrator plate. Layout in a small, even layer on the trays of the dehydrator, which has been covered with a parchment paper until the quinoa is fully cooked.

3. For 6-8 hours, dehydrate at 135, until the strawberries and quinoa are completely safe.

4. Put the coconut milk powder and coconut flakes in an airtight jar or pocket.

(At Camp)

1. Place a portion of the quinoa porridge in a small pot and add water to cover. Simmer for 10-15 minutes or until the quinoa is tender.

10. Sheepherder's Breakfast

Prep/Total Time: 30 min. servings 8

354 calories

Ingredients

*   3/4 lb. bacon strips, chopped finely

- 1 medium onion, chopped

- 30 ounces 1 package frozen hash brown shredded potatoes, thawed

- 8 eggs large

- 1/2 tsp salt

- 1/4 tsp pepper

- 1 cup cheddar cheese shredded

Directions

1. Cook the bacon & onion over med heat in the large skillet until the bacon is crispy. Drain, reserving 1/4 of a cup of pan drippings.

2. Stir the hash browns. Uncovered, cook it until the base is golden brown, around 10 minutes, over med heat. Turn the potatoes. Build eight equally distributed wells in the potato mixture using the spoon's back. In each well, break One egg. Use salt & pepper to sprinkle.

3. Cook, sealed, on low for around 10 minutes until the eggs are ready and the potatoes are soft. Sprinkle it with cheese; allow to stand until you have melted the cheese.

Chapter 3: Lunch & Dinner Recipes

Lunch and dinner are the most important meals of a day no matter you are at home or in a camp. The chapter enlists some of the easiest recipes that can be made while camping

1. Campfire Skillet Cornbread

Prep Time: 5 min Cook Time: 20 min Serving: 8

Per serving kcal: 127

Ingredients:

- 1 tbsp Baking powder
- ½ Cup Flour
- 1 Cup Med grind cornmeal
- 1/2 tbsp Oil
- 1 Egg
- 1 cup Milk
- ½ tsp Salt
- 2 tbsp Honey

Directions:

1. Combine the flour, cornmeal, salt & baking powder in a wide bowl.

2. In dry ingredients, add the egg, honey & milk. Mix it till completely combined.

3. Heat oil in the cast-iron pan above the campfire. And coat its bottom, swirl. Place the batter in the pan, making sure all is in the even layer. Cover the pan with foil crimping a foil across the corners.

4. Cook for fifteen min on med-low heat, then step away from the heat & allow the bread to rest for an extra five min (also now covered). Cut it into slices & enjoy it.

Note

You can make basic cast iron skillet cornbread fast on the right over the campfire.

2. Drunken Cauliflower Tacos with Quick Pickled Red Onions

Prep Time: 5 min Cook Time: 20 min Serving: 6

Per serving kcal: 107

Ingredients:

Cauliflower Tacos

- 2 tbsp Cumin

- 1 head Chopped cauliflower

- 2 tsp Dried oregano

- 1/8 tsp Cayenne

- 1 tsp Sea salt

- 6 Corn tortillas

- 2 cloves Minced garlic

- 1 tbsp Olive oil

- ½ cup Lager

Quick pickled onions

- 2/3 Juiced limes

- 1 small Sliced red onion

Directions:

1. Prepare the fast-pickled onions: in a tiny bowl, add the lime juice, salt & onions. Have them stay for around 15 to 20 min, tossing per five min

2. Cook the cauliflower: put cumin, beer, salt, dried oregano, garlic & cayenne to the cauliflower in a pan. Carry to a boil fast. Boil till all the liquid has vaporized, stirring regularly. If the liquid has vaporized, put the olive oil and fry till the cauliflower is soft and brown at the beginning.

3. Heat the tortillas: Heat the tortillas when the cauliflower is frying. We do this for 1 tortilla now in the stove burner, rotating every 15-20 sec so that all sides are toasty. This may be completed on a campfire as well, or in the oven, if you're at home.

4. Assemble the tacos: fill every tortilla with the scoop of pickled red onions, cauliflower, and some extra toppings

Note

Equipment needed:

Fine knife + chopping board + tiny bowl + wooden spoon + camp stove

3. Sweet & Savory Grilled Tempeh

Prep Time: 30 min Cook Time: 5 min Serving: 4

Per serving kcal: 167

Ingredients:

- 8 oz Tempeh

- 2 tbsp Soy sauce

- 1 tbsp Apple cider vinegar

- 1/4 cup Maple syrup

Directions:

1. In a zip-lock plastic bag wide enough to carry the tempeh, mix the soya sauce, apple cider vinegar & maple syrup.

2. Slice your tempeh into four slices. With marinade, put them within a zip lock bag. Be sure that the slices of tempeh are equally coated & allow for at least thirty min to marinate.

3. Grill/barbecue the tempeh on the campfire or roast it with a hint of oil in the cast iron pan. Cook on both sides for 2 to 3 mins.

Note

Equipment needed:

Fine knife + chopping board + cups + spoons

4. Artichoke & Poblano Campfire Paella

Prep Time: 5 min Cook Time: 40 min Serving: 2

Per serving kcal: 300

Ingredients:

- 2 Poblano peppers

- 1 large Diced shallot

- 3 Green onions

- 3 cloves Roughly minced garlic

- ¼ cup Tempranillo

- 14 oz can Broth

- 14 oz can Halved & drained artichoke hearts

- ½ cup Rice

- Saffron pinch

- ½ tsp Salt

- 2 tbsp Olive

Directions:

1. Put the green onions, sausage & poblanos peppers directly on the fire on the grill pan, rotating periodically, till the onions & peppers are tender & crispy & the sausage is cooked completely. Take it from your grill. Cut your sausage into pieces of around 1/4 inch. Let the peppers to chill, extract the seeds, peel the skin off, & chop. Mince the green onions into bite-sized bits.

2. Put the cast iron pan straight on over fire on the barbecue/grill. To cover the bottom of the pan,

add plenty of oil & then place the shallots. Saute for 3 to 5 mins till it is smooth. Place the garlic & sliced sausage & sauté for around 30 sec, till the garlic is aromatic. Put the rice & cook for 2 to 3 mins, often mixing till the ends are only translucent. Place 1/4 cup red wine in the skillet, allow to vaporize. After that, put the broth. Add salt as well as a pinch of saffron to season. Mix well to spread all the ingredients equally, and then leave 20 to 30 mins to boil, undisturbed, till all the liquid has been absorbed.

3. To reheat, add to the skillet the sliced green onions, artichoke hearts & poblanos. At that moment, the paella on the bottom will start forming the Socarrat. You would start hearing the rice beginning to crackle within a few mins. That's the sign here that the dish is almost finished. To ensure that the Socarrat has formed, cook for another few mins.

4. Serve quickly.

Note

With tasty veggies & spices, this pan campfire paella could be made vegan/gluten-free.

5. Shakshuka

Prep Time: 5 min Cook Time: 20 min Serving: 2

Per serving kcal: 276

Ingredients:

- 1 Seeded & sliced red bell pepper

- 1 Diced small onion

- 3 cloves Chopped garlic

- 2 tsp Paprika

- Minced parsley

- 1/4 cup Feta cheese

- 14 oz can Diced tomatoes

- 1 tsp Cumin

- 1 Sliced & seeded poblano peppers

- Pepper & salt

- 1 tbsp Olive oil

Directions:

1. Warm oil over low heat in your pan. When the poblano, red bell peppers & onions are warmed, swirl to cover, & cook for five mins or color changes to brown, stirring if required. Put the paprika, cumin & garlic then cook for around thirty sec till it is fragrant.

2. Place the tomatoes as well as their juices. To allow the combination to thicken, lower the heat & boil for ten min.

3. Break the eggs into the sauce, uniformly spaced them apart. Cover & let the eggs boil till the whites are set, 5 to 7 mins. To allow them to cook completely, you may spoon that sauce on over top as required.

4. Top to taste. Serve with feta cheese, sliced parsley, and a couple of pieces of crusty bread.

Note

Equipment needed:

Fine knife + chopping board + wooden spoon + utensils for serving

6. Campfire Pizza Margherita

Prep Time: 25 min Cook Time: 15 min Serving: 2

Per serving kcal: 1150

Ingredients:

For the crust

- 1 packet Rapid rise yeast

- 1 cup Warm water

- 5 tbsp Olive oil

- 2 ½ cups Flour

- 2 tsp Salt

Toppings

- 1 large Sliced into 1/4-inch tomato

- 8 oz Cut into 1/4-inch rounds mozzarella ball

- 2 tbsp Cut into ribbons fresh basil

- 1/2 cup Tomato sauce

Directions:

1. Add the yeast, salt & flour into a food processor or bowl. To split the ingredients, gently combine with a fork.

2. To dry ingredients, add the hot water and 2 tbsp of oil & combine with the fork till the ingredients start to shape the dough.

3. Knead your dough a couple of times so all the components are very well combined & the dough stays together.

4. Cover your dough for twenty mins & allow it to rise.

5. Turn it out on a chopping board once your dough has risen, then split the dough into 2 separate parts.

6. In a 10-inch cast-iron pan, put 1 tbsp oil to make the crust & swirl to cover the top. Put one of the dough halves within the pan, push & press the dough into the pan's sides with the fingers. Sprinkle 1/2 tbsp of oil with the sides of the pan.

7. Put the pan at suitably high heat on a grate on the campfire/camp stove. Cook for 3 to 5 mins, till the bottom has tightened up & starts to change to a golden brown.

8. Remove the pan from the heat & put it on a heat-safe surface. The pan would be hot, so stay aware of the next few stages.

9. Take a crust out from the pan by using 2 tongs & flip it so that the pan's non-cooked part is face-down.

10. Split tomato sauce 1/4 cup over on the top of the pizza, after this layer the minced tomatoes & mozzarella. Season the top with basil.

11. Bring the pizza to the stove/campfire. Cook the pizza till the bottom becomes golden brown for 3 to 5 mins. After some mins, remove the foil or lid when the cheese is melted to allow the steam to escape for the rest of the cooking period,

12. Remove the pan from the oven, move the pizza safely to a dish & repeat for the second half of the dough.

7. Dutch Oven Chicken Marbella

Prep Time: 5 min Cook Time: 45 min Serving: 4

Per serving kcal: 475

Ingredients:

- 1 cup Halved & pitted olives

- 1/4 cup Capers

- 1/2 cup Dry white wine

- 1 cup Chopped prunes

- 6 cloves Roughly minced garlic

- 2 tbsp Dried oregano

- 1 tsp Salt

- 2 Bay leaves

- 1/4 cup Red wine vinegar

- 1 tbsp Olive oil

- 4 tsp Brown sugar

- 4 Skin-on chicken thighs

Directions:

1. Marinate the chicken: put the bag in the freezer to marinate all ingredients except the brown sugar & oil. For at least six hrs. & up to 2 days, put in your icebox.

2. Prepare the campfire: twenty-seven prep coals. If you need to, you could use wood embers, although you'll have to measure the right heat ratio (you're looking for 220 c). When all the coals are fully prepared, knock them into just a plain pile & put them all on top of the Dutch

oven. This would produce the higher heat needed for browning.

3. Brown the chicken: in the Dutch oven, heat 1 tbsp of oil. The oil is ready & hot once the water drops sizzles as it hits the skillet. Take your chicken from marinade, then brush 1 tsp of brown sugar over both thigh's skin side. Brown the thighs' skin side at high temperature till the skin becomes crispy & its color changes to a deep golden brown, around 6-8 mins. Please turn to the other side for two mins to brown it.

4. Bake: turn off the Dutch oven heat. Put the marinade to the oven of Dutch & cover. Spread 18 coals equally on the lid and put nine coals in the oven of Dutch. Bake for thirty mins till the thighs are fully cooked & with there, juices run clear once stabbed with a knife.

5. Serve and enjoy with a few of a sauce spooned on the top, serve it over couscous, pilaf/rice.

8. Moroccan Chicken Couscous

Prep Time: 5 min Cook Time: 5 min Serving: 2

Per serving kcal: 665

Equipment

- Backpacking stove
- backpacking pot

Ingredients:

- 1 cup Chopped dried apricots
- 1 tsp Sea salt
- 2 tbsp Olive oil
- 1 packet True lemon
- ¼ cup Sliced almonds
- 7 oz packet Cooked chicken
- 5 oz Water
- 4 tsp Ras el Hangout
- ½ cup Couscous

Directions:

1. At home: in a resealable plastic bag, put the apricots, couscous, almonds, salt & raps el Hanout. Pack the packets of the chicken pouch, true lemon & olive oil.

2. At camp: in the cookpot, put ~5 oz of water & oil to a boil. Then put to the pot the apricots, couscous, spices, true lemon & nuts. To mix, give it a major shake, put to the chicken, then cover & take it from the heat. Let sit for five mins.

Note

Make it vegan/vegetarian

By swapping the chicken with the protein source like the TVP/soy curls, this could easily be turned vegetarian/vegan.

9. Sweet + Spicy Cashew Chicken Wrap

Prep time 3 min, Total time 3 minutes, Serving 2

Per serving Calories: 450kcal

Ingredients

- ½ cup-chopped Cashews

- 1 tsp Dried cilantro

- Salt

- 2 pkt-2 tbsp Honey

- 2 pkt-2 tbsp Mayo

- pkt 1-2 Sriracha

- 2 Tortillas/wraps

- 17 oz packet Cooked chicken

Directions

1. Place the cashews, sugar, mayo, Sriracha packs, coriander, and salt in a bag at home. Load the bag along with the cashews and the chicken pocket.

2. Drain the chicken if required at the camp. Add the chicken with the cashews, butter, Sriracha, cilantro, mayo and salt and stir to mix. Spoon the mixture of chicken onto the tortillas. Roll up burrito-style for them and enjoy.

10. Pie Iron Pizza Pockets

Prep time 30 min, cook time 15 min, Serving 4 pizza pockets

Per serving: kcal: 550

Ingredients

Pizza Dough

- 1 pkt Rapid rise yeast
- 2 tsp Salt
- 1 cup Warm water
- 2 tbsp Olive Oil
- 2 ¾ cups All-purpose Flour

Fillings

- 1 cup Shredded mozzarella cheese (Low moisture)
- 1 Diced green bell pepper
- 4oz can Sliced black olives (drained)
- 16 slices Pepperoni
- Oil
- ½ cup Pizza sauce

Directions

1. Make the dough: Stir together flour, salt, and yeast in mixing bowl. Add water and oil. Mix the ingredients with the help of a spoon/fork till the dough forms. If it appears too wet, add more flour, then knead till a ball form. Cover it and let it rise for 20 min. * Using pre-made

dough as an option.

2. Divide that dough into eight parts. Stretch n flatten that dough to roughly 4 and a half x 4 and a half-inch squares when working with the two pieces at a time.

3. Press the pie iron into the bottom plate with one square of the dough, after oiling it. Load the following ingredients: 2tbsp sauce, 1/4cup cheese, 1/4 bell pepper, 1oz olives, and 4pepperonis. Top it with the 2nd square of the dough. Close and lock pie iron.

4. Cook till the crust becomes golden brown; flipping is needed to assure even heat, over fire / on top of campfire embers. Depending on the campfire strength, the precise time would be different, but usually, this will probably take 2-3 min. Check it often.

5. Remove from heat, then unlock the pie iron thoroughly and turn out the pizza pocket.

6. With remaining ingredients, repeat. Be aware that while prepping subsequent pizza pockets, the Iron would be HOT. Wait till the Iron has been cooled / while reloading Iron, take extreme caution.

Notes

Pre-Trip Prep: Dough can be prepared ahead of time at home and packed in your refrigerator in a container. To make it easy to roll out, remove it from the cooler 30 min before cooking.

Shortcuts: You can use pre-made, store-bought dough instead of producing your pizza dough.

Chapter 4: Fish and Seafood

In this chapter, there are different recipes mentioned which can be enjoyed while camping.

1. Baja Style Fish Tacos

Prep time 10min, cook time 10min, Serving depends

Calories: 395kcal

Ingredients

- 1 cup Panko breadcrumbs

- 1 package Farm Organic Southwest (Earthbound, Chopped) Salad Kit

- 1/2 cup Flour

- 1/2-pound Snapper fillets

- 1/2 cup Grapeseed oil

- 6-8 Corn tortillas

- 1 tsp Salt

- 2 Eggs

- 1 Lime, quartered

Directions

1. **Preparation of breading station**: Crack eggs into a small bowl then beat them together. Then spread flour and panko onto 2plates (OR 2 sides of 1large plate).

2. **Bread the fish:** Chop the fish fillets into ½-¾inch strips. Sprinkle salt on the tops. Dredge every piece in the flour, dip in the egg for coating, let the excess drip off, and then coat in the panko. Set it aside.

3. **Frying of fish:** Line a plate along with a paper towel. Heat almost ½cup neutral-flavored oil in a high-sided pan. Once that oil is hot, now add fish 1piece at a time. Fry till breading is golden, and fish is cooked through, 30-60s on every side. Remove that fish as they end the cooking then place on a lined plate.

4. **Assembling of tacos:** Warm tortillas on stove / over a campfire. To make tacos, lay down a bed of greens from the salad kit, add in a piece or 2 of the fried fish, and top it with some of the included tomatillo dressing, additional cilantro, onions, and a squeeze of the lime.

2. Mediterranean Salmon in Foil Packets

Prep time 10 min, cook time 25 min, Serving 4

Per serving: Calories: 202kcal

Ingredients

- 1/2cup prepared pesto

- 1 Onion (chopped)

- 1 Halved Pint grape tomatoes

- 4 (almost 6 ounces each) Salmon fillets

- ½cup Crumbled feta cheese

Directions

1. Heat the oven to 350 F (180 C). Spray 4large pieces of the aluminum foil with the cooking spray.

2. Place every salmon fillet on the top of a piece of aluminum foil. Top every fillet with about 2 tbsp pesto, ¼ cup onion, ¼ tomatoes, and approximately 2 tbsp of feta cheese. There is no need for measuring ingredients - just use as much / as little as you'd prefer.

3. Seal aluminum foil packets through folding them over that fish and by pinching firmly to close it. Place foil packets on a large baking sheet then bake for approx. 25min. Fish is completed when it may flake easily with a fork.

Notes

If you're cooking for 2: Chop the ingredients in half, by using only 2salmon fillets. Cooking Directions remain the same.

3. Oregon Coast Campfire Paella

Prep time 15min, cook time 45min, Serving 2

Per serving: Calories: 700kcal

Ingredients

- 1 ½ C Broth

- 1 medium Onion (minced)

- 15 Cherry tomatoes

- 3 tbsp Olive Oil

- Saffron Big pinch

- 2 tsp Salt

- ½ tsp Paprika

- 4 cloves Garlic minced

- ½ tsp Red pepper flakes

- ½ cup Kenwood Vineyards Sauvignon Blanc

- For garnish Parsley

- 1 cup Short, grained rice

- 1-pound Seafood (mussels, shrimp, or mix)

Directions

1. Prepare seafood if you need - scrub mussels & debeard mussels, clams, and devein shrimp/prawns if not already. Place mussels & clams in the large bowl with cold water for soaking when you prepare the remaining ingredients.

2. Start campfire - over flames on high heat, you would be cooking, so there is no need to burn down the woods to the embers. Place the cast Iron onto the grill.

3. Measure 1 ½cups broth to a cup/bowl. Add saffron to broth and mix. Put aside. Mince the garlic & Dice the onion.

4. Once the fire is on, and hot is the skillet, add olive oil now followed by diced onion, red pepper flakes, and salt. Saute for almost 2minutes, till onion is beginning to be tender.

5. Add minced garlic & rice to skillet. Toast rice, mixing frequently, 2-3min / till it starts to be golden (not brown). Add wine and mix till rice absorb it, around 3min.

6. Add paprika, mixing briefly for coating rice & then add broth with saffron and roasted tomatoes. Now Give a big mix for distributing all the ingredients & then leave it. After 15min, add clams, mussels, and shrimp. Now Cook for around 15min further. The paella is finished once tender the rice is, all the liquid is absorbed, & you hear rice started "crackling" - the indicator that paella's forming Socarrat - wonderfully brown crust and crunchy that paella's known for.

7. Take out from the heat, then with parsley garnish it & enjoy.

Notes

Saffron can be expensive, but it also adds to the distinct paella flavor.

It is good to remember that the campfires aren't the heat sources (consistent) like kitchen stoves, so cooking time may be variable like how hot the fire is / how much the grill grate is close to the flame.

4. Chili Coconut Scallop Campfire Dinner

Prep time 5min, cook time 20min, Serving 4

Per serving: Calories: 177kcal

Ingredients

- 1 Red pepper

- 4 tbsp Butter

- 2 cups Carrots

- 4 tbsp Sweet chili sauce

- 2 cups Scallops

Directions

1. **Divide all the ingredients into 4:** Place every portion onto 2layers of the heavy-duty aluminum foil. Fold that foil to make a packet, then seal shut. You would have 4packets.

2. Place on campfire / BBQ and then grill for 15-20min, till everything is cooked.

3. Remove it and serve them with rice, French bread/noodles.

5. Fish & Vegetable Foil Dinner

Prep time 10min, cook time 10min, Serving 4

Per serving: Calories: 229kcal

Ingredients

- 1 bunch Asparagus

- 2 Bell peppers chopped

- 1 to 2 Lemons chopped into slices

- 1 Yellow squash

- 2 tsp Lemon juice

- Salt and pepper

- 1 Zucchini

- 4 frozen thawed Tilapia fillets

- Garlic powder

Directions

1. Place 4 bits of foil on the board. Each item should have a length of around 16 inches.

2. Wash out the asparagus spears and break the ends off. On every piece of foil, lay down 5 to 6 spears.

3. Wash & slice yellow squash & zucchini—Lay each slice 3 to 5 over the asparagus.

4. Along the asparagus sides, add sliced bell peppers.

5. Use pepper, salt, and garlic powder to sprinkle.

6. Place fillets of tilapia over the vegetables.

7. Sprinkle the lemon juice, around 1/2 tsp per fillet, over the fish top.

8. Using pepper, salt, and garlic powder to sprinkle. Then, over each fish top, spread 1/2 fresh lemon slices.

9. Wrap the foil around veggies & fish, making the packets

10. Cook on a high-set grill (about 400 to 450 degrees) on either side for 4-5 mins.

11. Remove them from the grill and open the packets carefully. Immediately serve.

6. Lemon-Dill Salmon Packets

Prep Time: 25 Serving: 4

Per serving Cal: 305

Ingredients:

- 1 Sliced med lemon

- 4 Salmon fillets

- 1/4 tsp Pepper

- 4 Sliced garlic cloves

- 4 Dill sprigs fresh

- 1/2 Med sliced onion

- 1/2 tsp Salt

- 1 tbsp Chopped fresh basil

- 1 tbsp Softened butter

Directions:

- Under med heat, arrange a grill/campfire. Distribute butter in the middle of each of the four bits of foil of double thickness. Put in the middle of 1 salmon fillet: season with pepper & salt. Season with onion, dill, garlic, basil & lemon on top. Around fillets, fold foil.

- Put packets over the grill/campfire on the grill grate. Cook till the fish quickly starts to flake with such a fork, eight to ten mins. Let the steam escape open safely.

7. Grilled Campfire Trout Dinner

Prep Time: 20 min Cook Time: 20 min Serving: 4

Per serving Cal: 362

Ingredients:

- 2 Dressed trout

- 1 Halved & sliced small onion

- 4 Lemon slices

- 1/8 tsp Pepper

- 1/4 tsp Salt

- 4 Bacon strips

Carrots:

- Dash pepper

- 1 tbsp Butter

- Wedges of lemon

- 1/8 tsp Salt

- 4 Thinly sliced med carrots

Directions:

1. Till slightly cooked and not crisp, cook bacon; drain. Put every trout on the heavy-duty foil of double thickness. put the onion & lemon in the cavities of trout, season with pepper & salt. Cover the bacon with the trout. Fold the foil strongly throughout the trout & seal.

2. Put the carrots on the heavy-duty foil of double thickness; toss with pepper & salt. Put dots of butter on top of the filling. Fold the foil firmly throughout the carrots & seal.

3. Grill the carrots, wrapped, for ten min on med heat. To grill, put packets of trout; cook 20 to 25 mins longer or till carrots & fish flakes are soft easily with a fork. Serve with wedges of lemon.

Note

With this easy procedure that maintains the fish moist, your fresh catch can taste much better. Carrots are a perfect accompaniment; cook in a separate package of foil.

8. Cajun Shrimp Foil Packets

Prep Time: 10 min Cook Time: 10 min Serving: 4 packets

Per serving kcal: 854

Ingredients:

- 25 Uncooked shrimp

- 4 Washed & cubed red potatoes

- 1/2 cup Melted butter

- 1 tbsp Cajun

- 1-pound Smoked sausage sliced into chunks

- Pepper & salt

- 1/2 cup   Chicken broth

- 18 pieces Corn on the cob

Directions:

1. Preheat the grill to 400 degrees. You could do this in the oven at about the same temp.

2. Divide up potatoes, corn, sausage & shrimp b/w four.

3. Sprinkle melted butter & around 2 tbsp chicken broth on every foil packet.

4. Season equally & nicely with salt, Cajun & pepper.

5. Firmly wrap foil packets by bending both sides on over components & firmly bending ends on over seam.

6. Cook 30 to 40 mins or till potatoes have become soft, turning when half-way thru

7. Be cautious, opening each packet to confirm for doneness. The vapor within it is very hot.

Equipment

- Outdoor Barbecue Grill

Notes

Several people have noticed that the potatoes don't get cooked. Our readers also suggested microwaving/boiling the potatoes for just one minute or two before putting on the packages. With potatoes having completed, we have not had an issue, but this is certainly a choice for those worried about it. Another choice will be to split the potatoes into small so that they cook quicker.

9. Shrimp Boil Foil Packets

Prep Time: 5 min Cook Time: 10 min Serving: 2

Per serving kcal: 520

Ingredients:

- 1 med Sliced courgette

- 1/2 lb. Uncooked shrimp

- 2 Andouille sausage

- 1 tsp Seasoning Cajun

- 4 Minced garlic cloves

- Chopped fresh parsley

- 1 tsp Old Bay

- 4 tbsp Butter

- 1 Sliced in 8 pieces corn ear

Directions:

1. For each package, tear an 18 "strip of heavy-duty plastic, including a 16" sheet of bakery release paper within each. layer the bakery release paper on top of the foil.

2. B/w the 2 foil sheets, split the corn, courgette, chopped garlic, spices, shrimp, & butter.

3. Carry 1 of the short sides of the foil to reach the other to shape the packages. After this, crimp along all the sides to seal.

4. Cook the packages for around eight mins on a barbecue, turning often.

5. Take it off the grill & allow it to cool a little bit. Smartly open the packets-they would be filled with hot steam. Season with new/fresh parsley.

10. Campfire Grilled Fish Tacos with Spicy Corn Salsa

Prep Time: 10 min Cook Time: 20 min Serving: 6

Per serving kcal: 133

Ingredients:

For the Fish

- 1 tbsp olive oil

- ½ Lime

- 1 tsp Chili powder

- 2 Snapper fillets 2/other mild, white fish

- 1/2 tsp Cumin

- 1/2 tsp Salt

  For the spicy corn salsa

- 1/2 small Red onion

- 1 Jalapeno

- ½ Lime

- Handful cilantro

- Salt

- 1-2 ears Cob corn

To serve

- Warmed over the fire 6 tortillas

- Kettle chips

Directions:

1. Begin the campfire/grill-this meal will be cooked over med-high heat.

2. Prepare the fish by brushing each side with the cumin, chili powder & salt, & by pressing half a lime on over the fillets and the drizzle of olive oil.

3. Put the corn & jalapeno on a grill when the fire is set. Grill for around ten min, often rotating, till soft. Remove & set aside to chill gradually.

4. In the wire grill tray, put the fish. Put the fish just on the grill & cook for around three mins, after this turn & cook two minutes further. For one min or two, remove and allow the fish to rest.

5. Create the salsa, whereas the fish is frying. Cut the maize off the cob, strip the jalapeno's blackened skin, cut, mince the onion thinly, & chop the coriander. Put it all in the bowl & squeeze half a lime into the liquid. Put salt.

6. With the heated tortillas, fish, avocado & corn salsa, make the tacos. Serve it.

Notes

Equipment needed:

Large plate + bowl + wire grill tray + chopping board + knife + utensils for serving

Chapter 5: Chicken, Beef, Pork, And Lamb

Meat lovers are everywhere. Those who love meat during camping would love to see the recipes enlisted in this chapter

1. Grilled Chicken Fajita Skewers

Prep time 6-7 min, cook time 15 min, Serving 4

Per serving: Calories: 195kcal

Ingredients

- 3 Tbsp Chili powder

- 2 tbsp Cumin

- 1/2 tsp Salt, to taste

- 1 lb. Cubed Chicken Breast

- 1 Bell Pepper (Green) chopped in square slices

- 1/2 Tbsp Garlic powder

- 1 Red onion chopped into square slices

- 1 Bell Pepper (Yellow) chopped in square slices

- 1 Bell Pepper (Red) chopped in square slices

Directions

1. Mix the garlic powder, chili powder, cumin, & salt in a large bowl.

2. to the spice blend, Add the cubed chicken and toss till it is coated.

3. Alternate among chicken, onions, and peppers, on the skewer before each skewer is complete.

4. Sprinkle the skewers with some more salt.

5. Grill 4-5 minutes on either side or till chicken is cooked completely, over med-high heat.

6. Serve your fajitas with tortillas of corn or flour, sour cream, guacamole, salsa, and something else you want.

2. Pizza Grilled Cheese

Prep time 10 min, cook time 20min, Serving 4

Per serving: Calories: 520kcal

Ingredients

- 1/4 cup Shredded parmesan cheese

- 1/2 cup Marinara sauce more needed for dipping

- 1/2 cup Pepperoni diced

- 3 tbsp Butter softened

- 1/4 cup Mozzarella cheese

- 1/2 tsp Italian seasoning

- 8 French bread slices

- 1/4 cup Ricotta cheese

- 1/8 tsp Garlic powder

Directions

1. On both of French bread slices, spread the butter. Place butter side down on a baking sheet covered with Silpat. Spread sauce on slices of French bread. Mix the remaining ingredients to and place on French bread slices. Place French bread slices on top of each other to create 4 sandwiches. Gently pat 1 tsp of parmesan cheese on each side of the sandwich. Place a preheated frying pan on medium to high heat for 5 minutes on each side or until edges are crispy. Transfer bake to a baking sheet and continue to bake in a preheated 400-degree oven until all cheese is melted. Serve with additional marinara sauce.

3. Spicy teriyaki grilled steak kebabs

Marinade 6hr, cook time 30 min, Serving 6

Per serving: Calories: 692kcal

Ingredients

- 1 ½ inch piece 1 Red pepper chopped

- 1 ½ pieces 1 Onion chopped

- 1-inch slices 3 to 4 Zucchini chopped

- 1cup Soy sauce

- 1-inch pieces 3 cups Fresh pineapple chopped

- 1cup Brown sugar

- ⅔cup Water

- 8 to 10 Wooden/metal skewers

- 1 tsp Freshly grated ginger

- ½cup Rice wine vinegar

- 1 ½ pieces 1Green pepper chopped

- 1 tbsp Corn-starch

- 4 cloves Garlic minced

- 1 ½ inch cube 2 lbs. Sirloin steak chopped

- 1 tsp Red pepper flakes

Directions

1. Mix the soy sauce, water, sugar, vinegar, garlic, red pepper flakes, and ginger in a small bowl till the sugar dissolves.

2. In a big zip lock freezer container, put the steak cubes and add 1/3 of the marinade mixture into them. Put and marinate in the refrigerator for at least 6 hrs., though ideally overnight.

3. Add the leftover marinade to a saucepan and stir in the corn starch till it is combined. Carry the sauce to the boil and cook for 20 mins or before the sauce thickens. Just set aside.

4. Heat the grill to a med-high temperature. Thread the skewers with steak, onions, zucchini, peppers, and pineapple alternately. After each rotation, grill the skewers 3 TO 4 mins per side (or till the perfect), brushing glaze over the top. Remove the skewers and leave for 10 minutes to rest. Brush it with thickened teriyaki sauce and sprinkle it with the sesame seeds.

5. Be sure to soak the wooden skewers for 30 minutes (or use metal). This benefits them because they do not burn even on a hot grill.

4. How to Make Campfire Pizza

Prep time 5min, cook time 15min, Serving 1

Per serving: Calories: 1634kcal

Ingredients

- Pepperoni mushrooms, veggies, or whatever toppings.

- 1 jar Pizza sauce

- Refrigerated pizza dough/frozen pizza dough one tube

- 2 cups Mozzarella cheese

Directions

1. Oil the cast-iron pan (or pizza stone, baking sheet, etc.)

2. The refrigerated dough is taken and spread into the pan.

3. Put on a fireplace or a BBQ. Cook until you've browned the rim.

4. From the fire, remove it & flip the crust into the pan.

5. Place the toppings on, brush it with pizza sauce, and then fill with cheese.

6. Back to the fire and cook till the crust underneath is complete, and the toppings are hot.

7. Enjoy.

Notes

Nutritional data will depend on what your toppings are.

5. Cilantro Lime Grilled Chicken Tacos

Prep time 5 min, cook time 25 min, Serving 4

Per serving kcal: 275

Ingredients

Cilantro Lime Marinade:

- Limes 2 juice
- 1 tsp Chili powder
- 1 tbsp Oil
- 2 tbsp Chopped cilantro
- ½ tsp Garlic powder
- 1 tsp Salt
- ½ tsp Ground coriander
- 4 (about 1 lb.) Chicken thighs (boneless + skinless)
- 1 tsp Cumin

Taco Assembly:

- Cilantro
- Pico de Gallo
- Cheese
- Tortillas

Directions

1. **Preparation of marinade:** inside the small bowl, blend the lime juice with zest, oil, spices,

2. and cilantro. Place chicken in a sealable container / Tupperware and pour over the marinade, shake to ensure that chicken is uniformly coated. Marinate it for least 30 min up to 2hr (1hr is better).

3. For grilling, prepare the grill or set up a campfire.

4. From that marinade, remove chicken and put it on the grill. Cook till the internal temp becomes 165F, turning as done to maintain even cooking (on each side for approximately 5-8 min). Remove from heat and cut into bite-sized bits.

5. To assemble the Layer chicken, cheese, Pico de gallo, fresh cilantro, and tacos into tortillas (warmed grill if you prefer).

6. Pineapple Chicken Kabobs

Prep time 10 min, cook time 10 min, Serving 4

Per serving kcal: 275

Ingredients

For the marinade:

- 1 tsp Salt

- ½ cup Chopped cilantro

- 2 tsp Minced Ginger

- 1 Lime, juiced

- 1 tbsp Honey

- ¼ cup Olive Oil

To build the skewers:

- Chicken (boneless + skinless thighs work best), cut into 1-inch pieces, ½ lb.

- Red onion (cut into 1inch pieces), 1 medium

- Pineapple wedges (chop into 1inch cubes)

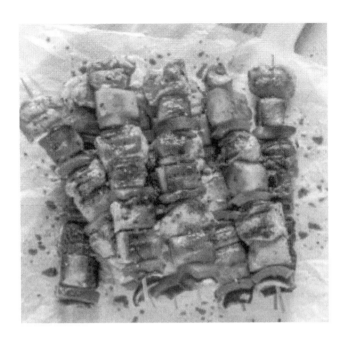

Directions

1. Combine your marinade ingredients in a wide bowl / in a ziplock container.

2. Add chicken to marinade and mix to coat it. Cover / lock the container and marinate for up to 24hrs 1hr or at least at an hr. If you're going to marinate longer than an hour, bring it back in your cooler.

3. Heat the grill, campfire going in the meantime.

4. By threading that chicken and veggies onto your skewers, create the kabobs. Brush it with a bit of oil.

5. Grill your kabobs on medium-high - high flame, rotating them regularly so that they cook uniformly till the chicken is cooked thru.

6. Remove it from the grill

Notes

Your choice seasoning: Bell peppers, poblano, jalapeños, or serrano peppers.

Put leftovers for food preservation and position them overnight in a fridge. In the morning, cut up the brats n peppers then blend them with eggs to produce a perfect scramble.

7. Cast Iron Brats with Peppers & Onions

Prep time 5 min, cook time 20 min, Serving 4

Per serving: Calories: 770 kcal

Ingredients

- Sandwich rolls/buns + mustard to serve

- 1 Yellow onion (cut into half-moons)

- 1 Red bell pepper (deseeded n cut lengthwise)

- 1 tsp Salt

- 1 lb. Bratwurst

- 2 tbsp Olive Oil

- 1 Poblano pepper (deseeded n cut lengthwise)

Directions

1. On campfire grill (or camp stove), preheat a cast-iron pan over medium heat. Apply the oil, then the peppers, onions, and salt. Cook till they just begin to be tender, for few mins, then incorporate the bratwurst, nestling them in veggies so that they come into interaction with the pan.

2. Switch the brats and occasionally mix the veggies till brats are cooked through (160°F internal temp), 15 to 20 min.

3. Turn off the heat, then divide the sandwich rolls between the brats n veggies.

4. Top it off with mustard and have fun.

Notes

You can use fresh pineapple - either whole pineapple. Alternatively, canned pineapple can be used.

8. Sweet Horseradish Glazed Ribs

Prep Time: 10 min Cook Time: 2 hrs. Serving: 8

Per serving Cal: 690

Ingredients:

- 2 tbsp Honey

- 1 to ½ tsp Divided salt

- 3 cups Unsweetened juice of apple

- 1/4 cup Ready drained horseradish

- 1 to 1/2 tsp Divided coarsely ground pepper

- Baby pork back ribs three racks

- 1 jar Apricot preserves

Directions:

- Oven preheated to 325 degrees. Remove the thin membrane from the ribs & discard it if required. Toss the salt & pepper over the ribs with one tsp each. Move, bone side down, to a big shallow roasting skillet; add juice/beer. Cook, wrapped, for 2 to 3 hours, till tender.

- After that, in a blender, add the horseradish, puree preserves, honey, leftover salt & pepper, & liquid smoke if wanted.

- Ribs drain. On a wide sheet of aluminum foil, put one rib rack. Rub with a combination of apricot-horseradish; cover firmly. Repeat for the ribs that remain. Put it for up to two days in the refrigerator.

- Under med heat, set a grill/campfire. Remove the foil from the ribs; grill till browned, 10 to 15 mins, turning sometimes.

Note

Roast the ribs, cover them and finish with a nice, savory sauce on the grill/campfire if you choose to prepare them before camping.

9. BBQ Chicken Quesadillas

Prep Time: 5 min Cook Time: 25 min Serving: 2

Per serving kcal: 722

Ingredients:

- 2 Skinless & boneless chicken thighs

- 2 Limes

- ¼ cup Barbecue sauce

- ½ tsp Salt

- 1 cup Chopped Colby jack

- 1 tbsp Cooking oil

- 1 tbsp Butter

- 1/4 cup Coriander

- To serve: avocado salsa & sour cream

- 4 large Flour tortillas

- small ½ Red onion

Directions:

- Finely chop the red onion in-home (roughly 2 days before the date) and put it in the resealable bag. Put the two-lime juice & salt, mix & refrigerate it.

- Place some cooking oil in the cast-iron pan at camp. Pat your chicken thighs on each side to dry & salt them. Put the thighs to the hot pan & fry till brown, 6 to 8 mins on 1 side. On the other hand, flip & finish cooking till cooked, 2 to 4 mins.

- Move the chicken and cut this into bite-sized parts on a chopping board. Move the bits to the bowl & put the coriander & barbecue sauce. Drain your red onions & put half of them to the chicken combination. Toss it to coat.

- Wipe the pan out & put the butter to it. Assemble directly into the pan for every quesadilla; the bottom tortilla, half the chicken combination, ¼ cup shredded cheese, another ¼ cup shredded cheese, as well as a second tortilla. Cook till its color changes to golden brown at the bottom, 2 to 4 mins, then turn. Cook for another 2-3 mins, till golden brown on the second side as well as the cheese, is melted.

- Season with further coriander & pickled red onions. Serve sliced avocado & salsa

Note

"These" gourmet "quesadillas are mostly the ideal camping lunch, mixing pan-fried chicken, BBQ sauce, jack cheese, red onions tangy pickled & melty Colby.

10. Grilled Bánh Mì with Quick Pickled Vegetables

Prep Time: 10 min Cook Time: 15 min Marinate: 2 hrs. Serving: 4

Per serving kcal: 414

Equipment

- Instant read thermometer
- chimney starter

Ingredients:

- ¼ tsp Ground ginger
- 1 tbsp Soy sauce
- ½ lb. Pork loin
- 1 tbsp Fish sauce
- ¼ tsp Salt
- 4 Sandwich rolls
- Mayo
- Quick pickled veggies
- 1 to 2 Jalapeno
- 2 tbsp Honey
- Fresh coriander

Quick pickled veggies

- ¼ tsp Salt
- ¼ cup Water
- ½ Daikon radish
- ⅓ cup Rice vinegar
- 1 Big carrot
- 1 tbsp Sugar

Directions:

Home

- Marinate your pork at home & create the rapid-pickled veggies.

- To prepare the marinade of pork: add the soy sauce, honey, fish sauce, salt & ground ginger in a tiny bowl & stir to mix. In a zip lock packet, put the pork loin & place the sauce further into the packet. Marinate for at least one hour.

- To prepare the pickled veggies: allumette the daikon radish & carrot and put them in a glass jar. Mix the rice vinegar, water, salt & sugar together in a tiny bowl. Place on the veggies & close the jar. Leave it for at least one hour, or place for up to a few days in the refrigerator.

Camp

- Make ready the fire at camp. You want med heat. From the marinade, take the pork & put it on the grill/barbecue. Grill/barbecue on one side for five min, then turn & grill/barbecue for 3 further minutes. Take it from the barbecue/grill, cover, & allow rest for around three minutes.

- Grill/barbecue the rolls of sandwich, if required, meanwhile. Cut the chiles & cucumber thinly. Sliced into small slices once the pork has rested.

- Sprinkle mayo on all sides of the rolls of the sandwich to arrange the sandwiches. Split the pork & toss with fresh coriander, cucumber, pickled veggies & sliced jalapenos b/w the sandwiches.

Note

These campfires Bánh mì brings sandwiches to such a different level: smoky, light baguette bread, spicy jalapenos, tangy pickled veggies & sweet pork.

11. Camping maple sriracha chicken kabobs

Prep Time: 10 min Cook Time: 15 min Serving: 1

Per serving Cal: 127

Ingredients:

- 1 Cubed red bell pepper

- 1/4 cup Maple syrup

- 1/4 cup Soy sauce

- 1 Cubed pineapple

- 1 tbsp Sriracha sauce

- 2 large Cubed chicken breasts

Directions:

1. In a big plastic bag resealable, put the chicken breasts cubed.

2. Mix the maple syrup, sriracha sauce & soy sauce.

3. Place on the top of the chicken & massage it through the chicken.

4. Marinate in an icebox for a time of fifteen mins to 24 hrs.

5. Soak the wooden skewers underwater for ten mins when the chicken is marinated.

6. After this, skewer the red bell pepper, pineapple & chicken pieces

7. Grill the chicken till fully cooked around ten minutes.

8. Serve it.

12. Camping Dutch oven chicken and dumplings

Prep Time: 20 min Cook Time: 1 hr. Serving: 1

Per serving Cal: 49

Ingredients:

- 4 Sliced celery ribs

- 3 med Sliced carrots

- 2 tsp Divided rubbed sage

- 1 cup Minced onion

- 3 cups Water

- 3 cups Biscuit

- 1 tsp Celery seed

- 1 tbsp Chopped fresh parsley

- 1/4 tsp Pepper

- 1 Broiler

- 3/4 cup + 2 tbsp Milk

- 1 tsp Salt

Directions:

1. Put the water as well as the chicken in the Dutch oven. Carry to a simmer & cover.

2. Lower the heat to boil; cook for around 30 minutes till the chicken is soft.

3. Take the chicken from the kettle; take the cube & bone.

4. Return the chicken, celery, onion, seed of celery, carrots, pepper, salt & 1 tsp of sage to the kettle.

5. Carry to a simmer.

6. Lower the heat.

7. For around 45 to 60 mins simmer & cover.

8. Mix the biscuit combination, parsley milk, and leftover sage for dumplings to shape the stiff batter.

9. Drop the tablespoonfuls within the combination of boiling chicken.

10. For around fifteen mins, cover & boil.

11. Serve right away.

13. Camping mac n cheese recipe

Prep Time: 20 min Cook Time: 20 min Serving: 1

Per serving kcal: 493

Ingredients:

- Salt & pepper & salt

- 1 ½ cups dry Elbow macaroni noodles

- 1 ½ cup Shredded cheese

- 1 package Sliced in one-inch rounds kielbasa

- ¼ - ½ cup Milk

- 8-10 oz Jarred alfredo sauce

Directions:

1. Cook kielbasa in a big cast iron pan. Drain the extra fat.

2. Cook pasta as per the product Directions in a separate oven. In cool water, wash & drain. At home, you can even cook noodles. To avoid the cooking process, store them in the cooler in a zip lock bag and shock them with cold water.

3. To make a sauce, add alfredo sauce, noodles, milk & cheese. Sprinkle with pepper & salt.

4. Steam for 5-10 minutes on a grill over campfire coals, stirring periodically before the cheese is thoroughly melted.

5. Take it from the heat & quickly serve.

14. Hawaiian BBQ Pork Walking Taco

Prep Time: 15 min Serving: 24

Ingredients:

- Pineapple salsa

- Chips Small bags

- Pork Byron for BBQ

- Chopped lettuce

- Minced Chopped cilantro

- Sour cream

- Chopped cheese

Directions:

1. As per the directions on a package, warm the pork BBQ.

2. Open the chips packet & crush it into tiny parts.

3. To make it very durable, roll down both sides of the packet.

4. Place the pork BBQ, shredded lettuce, shredded cheese, sour cream, pineapple salsa & coriander on top of the chips.

15. Tzatziki Chicken Skewers

Prep Time: 30 min Cook Time: 10 min Serving: 2

Per serving kcal: 527

Equipment

- Skewers

- Basting Brush

- Heat Resistant Gloves

Ingredients:

- 1/2 cup Prepared tzatziki

- 1 Lemon juice

- 2 tbsp Olive oil

- 1 Chopped red onion

- 1/2 tsp Salt

- 1/2 tsp Garlic powder

- 4 Sliced in 1 piece of boneless skinless chicken thighs

- 14 Cherry tomatoes

- 1 tbsp Dried oregano

- 1 small Sliced into 1/4" moons courgette

Tzatziki sauce

- 1/4 tsp Salt

- ¼ Chopped & removed seed cucumber

- 1 tbsp Chopped fresh mint

- 2 cloves Finely minced garlic

- 1/2 cup Greek yogurt

Directions:

1. In the bowl, combine the lemon juice, olive oil, garlic powder,1/2 tsp salt & oregano. Put your chicken & coat it. Leave aside to marinate for thirty min (up to two hrs.), tossing often.

2. To make tzatziki (it is necessary to make it ahead):

3. Blotting extracts extra moisture from the mined cucumber with the towel. Put the Greek yogurt, cucumber, garlic, salt, & mint in a tiny bowl and then stir to mix.

4. If completed ahead of time, cover & put in your freezer.

5. For grilling, arrange a barbecue or a campfire.

6. Thread into skewers with both the vegetables & chicken.

7. Put the skewers just on the grill grate & grill, rotating every several mins so that both sides cook equally. It will take the chicken 3 to 5 mins to cook on each side, and it will take between 10 to 12 mins for the vegetables.

8. Remove the skewers. For dipping, serve with tzatziki.

Notes

Without any side dishes, nutrition is based on two servings

16. Chicken Pad Thai

Prep Time: 5 min Cook Time: 15 min Serving: 4 packets

Per serving kcal: 571

Ingredients:

- ¼ cup Peanuts chopped

- 2 tbsp Sesame oil

- 1 large Cut into cubes chicken breast

- ⅔ cup Pad Thai sauce

- ½ cup Cilantro chopped

- 1 Diced small onion

- ¼ tsp Salt

- 2 Beaten eggs

- 7 oz Pad Thai noodles

- ½ cup Green onions sliced

   Pad Thai Sauce

- 1 tbsp Fish sauce

- 2 tbsp Lime juice

- 2 tbsp Soy sauce

- 2 tbsp Brown sugar

- 1 tbsp Chili-garlic sauce

- 2 tbsp Rice vinegar

Directions:

1. Carry a kettle of water to a simmer. Switch off the heat when the water is simmering & submerge your noodles for around 8 to 10 mins. Noodles get finished Once they become soft; however, "al dente."

2. In the meantime, heat two tsp of oil of sesame in a med saucepan. Put the onions, chicken & salt when it is warmed. Saute till the chicken is completely cooked as well as the onions tend to brown.

3. Place your chicken to 1 side of the skillet, reduce the heat. After this, put the eggs to pan, mixing them constantly to scramble.

4. Use tongs to lift your noodles it out their soaking water after the noodles are finished (see stage 1), the chicken is cooked over, as well as the eggs get scrambled. To the pot, put the noodles after this place in pad Thai sauce. To coat your noodles, mix.

5. Season with fresh coriander, green onions, & minced peanuts.

Chapter 6: Father/Son- Daughter

Here are some amazing recipes that can be easily cooked by father/son-daughter.

1. Zesty Mango Guacamole

Prep Time: 5 minutes, Total Time: 5 minutes, 4 servings

Nutrition (Per Serving): Calories: 174kcal

Ingredients

- 1/8 tsp Salt

- 1 Mango

- 2 tbsp - chopped Cilantro

- 1 Lime

- Tortilla chips

- 2 Avocados

- ¼ tsp Tajin seasoning/ Taco seasoning

Directions

1. In ½-inch bits, slice the avocado. Slicing the avocado in half is the best way to do this, cutting the seed, and then using the knife to grade the avocado into pieces (be cautious not to break through the skin). To scrape the avocado out of a cup, use a spoon.

2. Chop the mango into ½-inch bits. This is what I came to do from watching

3. With the avocado, apply the mango bits to the dish.

4. Cut the lime in half and squeeze it into the cup with the liquid. Apply the seasoning to the tajin and salt to taste. Toss and eat with tortilla chips instantly.

Notes

Adapted from Mother Nature Network

2. Trail Mix Bliss Balls

Prep Time: 10 minutes, Cook Time: 5 minutes, 8 bites

Nutrition (Per Serving): Calories: 118kcal

Ingredients

- 3 tbsp -dried Cranberries

- 1/4 cup Cashews

- 3 tbsp Pepitas

- 10 dates (pitted and soaked in water for 10 minutes)

Directions

1. Process the dates and cashews in a Vitamix or a food processor before a sticky dough emerges.

2. To build a ball, divide the dough into 8 equal parts and roll between your palms.

3. Spread on a flat surface (like a cutting board or plate) the pepitas and cranberries and roll the balls over them to cover.

4. Place the happy balls in the refrigerator in an airtight jar before you're about to reach the trail.

Notes

If you're using a high-powered blender like a Vitamix, you can skip soaking the cashews. Otherwise, give those a good soak warm water to soften them.

3. DIY Fruit Leathers

Prep Time: 15 minutes, Cook Time: 6 hours, Total Time: 6 hours 15 minutes

Ingredients

Strawberry rhubarb

- 1/4 cup Honey

- 3 cups-diced Strawberries

- 2 cups-diced & cooked Rhubarb

  Blueberry chia banana

- 2 cups Blueberries

- 2 small ripe & peeled Bananas

- 1/4 cup Chia seeds

- 5-10 dates (pitted)

Raspberry Peach

- 1/4 cup Honey

- 3 peaches (pitted & diced)

- 2 cups Raspberries

Directions

1. If needed, wash, peel, and extract any stems or pits. The fruit skin is highly nutritious, so the peel is always used (except for bananas, pineapples, oranges, etc.).

2. Put all the products with your sweetener of preference in a blender or food processor and blend until smooth. * When producing the version of the Strawberry Rhubarb: the rhubarb needs to be softened so that after dicing, put in a bowl with water to cover them and cook on medium to mild; we drain anything from the jar, water and all into the processor so that we do not waste the nutrients.

3. Optional step: We have noticed that it speeds up the drying period if you preheat the mixture in a pot before placing it in the dehydrator. Dump the combined mixture into a pot and run for 10-15 minutes on slow, stirring periodically.

4. Strip trays of the document on parchment. Spread on trays that are dehydrated. Make the puree thicker across the edges-about 1/4 "inch and 1/8" in the middle-as the sides dry faster.

5. Dry it for 6-8 hours at 145F/63C. Another approach to speed up the drying period is to evaluate and cut the wrap/paper within a few hours. They would be a little smooth and non-sticky to the touch when the leathers are dry. Until removing them from the trays, cause them to cool.

6. Roll the leather into a compact roll and cut it into your choosing lengths with a sharp knife. Cover saran wrap bits place them in airtight containers (such as zip lock bags), or vacuum seal.

Store in a position that is pleasant, dark & dry.

4. Chewy Chocolate Goji Granola Bar

Prep Time: 5 minutes, Cook Time: 20 minutes, Serving 6

Nutrition (Per Serving): Calories: 242kcal

Ingredients

- ½ cup Water

- 1 oz, chopped Dark chocolate

- 6 dates (pitted and roughly chopped

- 2 cups Rolled oats

- ¼ cup Goji berries

- ¼ cup Maple syrup

- 2 tbsp Chia seeds

- ¼ tsp Salt

- 1 tsp Vanilla extract

Directions

1. Preheat the furnace to 350.

2. Put the water, dates, chai seeds, maple syrup, vanilla, and salt into the dish in your food processor. Let it all soak for 5 minutes, then process until it is smooth (it is OK to have a couple of dates left, so you do not want huge chunks of them).

3. Over medium fire toast the oats in a heavy skillet until golden brown, around 5 minutes. Stir periodically to avoid them from burning to ensure even toasting.

4. Put the dark chocolate, oats, goji berries, and the date mixture in a medium mixing cup. Mix well with a spoon, so all the oats in the date mixture are fully coated.

5. Cover a loaf pan with parchment paper, 8.5' x 4.5' Spread the mixture into the pan uniformly, then push down on it to further compress it (for this, we used the bottom of a glass).

6. For 20 minutes, roast. Complete cold, then extract it from the pan and break it into six strips.

7. Cover them in parchment paper, bubble wrap, or tiny zip locks to render them waterproof, or stick them in your pack and go.

Notes

Measuring cups & spoons Food processor or blender Sharp knife + cutting board heavy-bottomed skillet 8.5" x 4.5" loaf pan Wooden spoon or spatula (Equipment Needed)

5. Pie Iron Pizza Pockets

Prep Time: 30 minutes, Cook Time: 15 minutes, Serving 4

Nutrition (Per Serving): Calories: 550kcal

Ingredients

- 2 tbsp Olive oil

- 2 tsp Salt

- 2 ¾ cups all-purpose flour

- 1 cup Warm water

- Pizza Dough

- 1 packet rapid rise yeast

Fillings

- 16 slices Pepperoni

- 1 cup low moisture shredded Mozzarella cheese

- Oil

- 1 green bell pepper, diced

- 4 oz can sliced-drained Black olives

- ½ cup Pizza sauce

Directions

1. Create the dough (it can be completed ahead of time.): Whisk together the starch, yeast, and salt in a mixing cup. Add the water and grease. Mix the products with a spoon or fork before a dough develops. If it is too warm, apply additional flour, then knead until a ball develops. Cover it and leave it to remain for 20 minutes. Using pre-made dough as an option.

2. Divide the dough into eight chunks. Stretch and flatten the dough into nearly 4 ½ x 4 ½-inch squares while dealing for two bits at a time.

3. Oil the pie iron and push onto the bottom plate with one square of pastry. Using the following ingredients: 2 teaspoons of sauce, ¼ cup of cheese, ¼ of bell pepper, 1 lb. of olives, and 4 pepperonis. Attach a second square of dough to the tip. Close & lock the iron for the pie.

4. Cook until the top is golden brown, flipping if needed to guarantee even flame, over the flames, or on top of your campfire embers. Depending on the campfire strength, the precise time would be unpredictable, but usually, this will probably take 2-3 minutes. Sometimes search.

5. Remove from the sun, then open the pie iron thoroughly and pull out the pizza bag.

1. With the remaining ingredients, repeat. Be aware that while prepping subsequent pizza pockets, the iron will be HOT. Wait till iron has cooled, or while reloading the iron, take extreme caution.

Notes

Pre-Trip Prep: The dough can be made at home ahead of time and stored in a container in your cooler. Remove from cooler 30 minutes before cooking to make it easier to roll out.

6. No-Bake Bourbon Peach Cobbler

Prep Time: 2 minutes, Cook Time: 18 minutes, Serving 2

Nutrition (Per Serving): Calories: 410kcal

Ingredients

- Optional Handful chopped almonds
- ½ cup Bourbon
- 1 tbsp Butter or neutral oil
- 3 ripe sliced Peaches
- 1 cup Granola
- 2 tbsp Sugar

Directions

1. Heat the oil or butter in a skillet (8- or 10-inches suits best) over medium heat. In

a single sheet introduces the peaches and cook for 2-3 minutes before they start to soften and brown in spots. Flip the peaches and cook an extra 2-3 minutes on the other hand.

2. Take the skillet off the fire (this may sound pointless, but if the flames from your campfire flare-up, it will keep the alcohol vapor from catching fire). Load the whiskey into the pan and place the pan back on the grill. To integrate and cover the peaches, apply 2 teaspoons of sugar, and mix well.

3. Continue to cook until the sauce decreases, and the peaches are tender, stirring regularly, for around 8-10 minutes. Remove from heat to create the crumble topping, scatter with 1 cup of granola (and sliced almonds if used) and serve immediately.

7. Chickpea Curry with Coconut Milk

Prep Time: 5 min Cook Time: 25 min Serving: 4

Per serving kcal: 358

Ingredients:

- Chopped cilantro
- 1 diced small onion
- 1 lime Cut into wedges
- 1 tbsp Garam masala
- 1 can Drained chickpeas
- 2 tbsp Tomato paste
- 1 tsp Salt
- 1 tsp Ground ginger
- 1 tsp Cinnamon
- 1 can Coconut milk
- 1 tsp Ground turmeric
- 1 tbsp Oil

Directions:

1. Under med heat, heat the oil in a pan & put the onions & fry

2. In the milk of coconut, put the chickpeas.

3. Cook on med-low heat, often mixing, for 10-15 mins, when that sauce thickens to desired taste.

4. In the meantime, ready the sides (see suggestions for serving).

5. With a lime squeeze, serve that chickpea curry & season it with sufficient of coriander.

Notes

Serving suggestion:

Serve with rice/cauliflower rice. Rice may be prepared ahead of time at home & reheated.

Another nice side is toasted naan-on over the open fire of your campfire/stove, often rotating using metal tongs till browned.

8. One-Pot Pasta Primavera

Prep Time: 5 min Cook Time: 20 min Serving: 2

Per serving kcal: 394

Ingredients:

- 2 oz Goat cheese

- 4 oz Pasta

- 2 cloves Garlic

- 1 yellow Summer squash

- 1 Courgette

- 4 oz Cherry tomatoes

- 1 tbsp Oil

- 1 tsp Salt

Directions:

1. Cut the squash & courgette into ¼-inch pieces—split half of cherry tomatoes. Chop the garlic.

2. In such a high-sided pan, warm the oil. When heated, place the saute & vegetables for around eight mins till the squash becomes tender. Take the veggies from the pan.

3. To the pan, put the pasta, salt, & just plenty of water to coat the pasta. Carry the water on med heat to a simmer & cook till the pasta is soft, around 10 minutes. To maintain even cooking, make sure to whisk regularly. You should still put a little more of the water if it boils off. When the pasta is ready, remove the pan from the fire.

4. To cover the pasta, mix within goat's cheese. Return to the pan put the veggies & combine to mix. Complete with a lemon squeeze, eat and enjoy.

Notes

Equipment Needed:

High sided pan + large chopping board + knife + bowls for serving.

9. Chickpea Breakfast Hash with Veggies

Prep Time: 5 min Cook Time: 15 min Serving: 2

Ingredients:

- 2 Eggs

- 1/8 tsp Cinnamon

- 1/2 tsp Cumin

- Cut half courgette

- 1 tbsp Oil

- 1 Drained chickpea

- 1/4 tsp Coriander

- 1/2 tsp Salt

Directions:

1. Add the oil in a pan on med-high heat on the campfire/camp stove till heated as well as shimmering. Add the peppers, onions, & courgette, then saute till around five mins begin to soften. Put the chickpeas & spices drained, then cook till the vegetable and chickpea are cooked & browned in patches, around ten minutes.

2. To make a well in the center of the skillet, transfer the chickpeas & vegetables to the skillet's sides. If the bottom of the skillet is looking rough, add kind of oil. Smash 2 eggs into a well & cook as you like.

3. Take the fire off the skillet & serve.

10. Mini S' mores

Time: 50 mins, Serve 4 dozen

1 piece: 145 calories.

Ingredients

- 2 c milk chocolate chips

- 1/2 c heavy whipping cream

- 14.4 ounces 1 package graham crackers, quartered

- 1 c marshmallow creme

- 7 ounces each 2 cartons milk chocolate for dipping

- 4 ounces melted white candy coating

Directions

1. In a bowl, put chocolate chips. Bring the cream to a boil in a tiny saucepan. Pour chocolate over; mix till its smooth. Cool it to room temp, or around 10 minutes, until the mixture achieves spreading consistency.

2. Spread over half the graham crackers with the chocolate mixture. Spread marshmallow cream over the remaining graham crackers; put on crackers covered in chocolate, pressing to stick to them.

3. In compliance with package instructions, melt dipping chocolate. Dip halfway each S' more into the chocolate dip; cause the excess to drip away. Place on waxed baking sheets lined with paper; let stay until the chocolate is ready to dip.

4. Drizzle tops with white melted candy coating if desired; let stand till finished. Store in the fridge in an airtight jar

11. Pizza Mountain Pies

Prep/Total Time: 10 mins, Serving 1

1 sandwich: 388 calories

Ingredients

- 1 tbsp butter, softened

- 2 white bread slices

- 1 tbsp pizza sauce

- 4 tbsp shredded mozzarella cheese, divided

- 4 pepperoni slices

- 1 tbsp green pepper chopped, optional

Directions

1. Spread the butter over slices of bread. Put one slice, buttered side down, in the sandwich iron. Spread with the pizza sauce; apply two tbsp of cheese, pepperoni & green pepper, if necessary. Top with the leftover slice of cheese and toast, butter side up.

2. Cook over some high campfire until the cheese is melted and golden brown, 3-6 mins, rotating periodically.

12. Easy Grilled Corn with Chipotle-Lime Butter

Prep: 5 mins, soaking Grill: 25 mins, servings 8

225 calories

Ingredients

- 1/2 tsp ground chipotle pepper
- 8 ears sweet corn in husks
- 1-1/2 tsp grated lime zest
- 1 tsp minced fresh cilantro
- 1/2 c butter, softened
- 1/2 tsp salt
- Optional Coarse sea salt

Directions

1. Cover the corn in a broad stockpot with cold water. 30 min to soak; drain. Grill the corn, covered, until tender, over med heat, rotating periodically, for 25-30 mins.

2. Combine the leftover ingredients meanwhile. Peel back the husks carefully; discard the silk. Spread the combination of butter over the corn

13. Blueberry-Cinnamon Campfire Bread

Total time: Prep: 10 min. Cook: 30 min. **Yield:** 8 servings.

266 calories

Ingredients

- 1 pound 1 loaf cinnamon-raisin bread

- 6 eggs large

- 1 cup milk/half-and-half cream

- 2 tbsp maple syrup

- 1 tsp vanilla extract

- 1/2 cup toasted chopped pecans

- 2 cups divided fresh blueberries

Directions

1. Prepare a campfire or low heat grill. Then on a greased dual thickness of foil heavy-duty (approximately 24x18 in.), place bread slices. Cover up the sides with foil, keeping the top exposed. Whisk in the eggs, milk, vanilla and syrup. Sprinkle it with nuts & 1 cup of blueberries; spill over the bread. Fold across the top corners, crimping to cover.

2. Put on a gas or a campfire for 30-40 mins before eggs are cooked clean. Remove from the heat; quit for 10 minutes to stand. Sprinkle with the leftover blueberries. If needed, top with extra maple syrup.

14. Campfire Hash

Total time: Prep: 15 min. Cook: 40 mins. **Yield:** 6 servings.

535 calories

Ingredients

- 1 onion, chopped

- 2 tbsp canola oil

- 2 minced garlic cloves

- 4 large potatoes, peeled & cubed (around 2 lbs.)

- 1 lb. smoked kielbasa or Polish sausage, halved and sliced

- 4 ounces 1 can, chopped green chiles

- 15 to 1/4 ounces 1 can, drained whole kernel corn

Directions

1. Cook and mix the onion in oil in a large ovenproof skillet over med heat under tender heat.

Put in garlic; simmer for 1 min longer. Add the potatoes. Cook it, uncovered, for 20 mins, frequently stirring.

2. Add the kielbasa; cook and mix for 10-15 mins, until the meat &potatoes are browned and tender. Stir in the corn and chiles; heat up.

Chapter 7: Mother/Son-Daughter

Camping is even more fun when you cook together. Below, some recipes are mentioned that are so easy that your kids can even help you out in preparing food.

1. Campfire Nachos

Prep time 5 min, cook time 12 min, Serving 6

Per serving: Calories: 452kcal

Ingredients

- 1 ½ cups Cheddar jack cheese shredded
- 4 ounces can Mild green chiles diced
- 11 ounces Tortilla chips
- 1 Cup Canned corn drained
- Olive oil
- 15 ounces can Black beans (rinsed n drained)
- ½ Diced Red bell pepper

Directions

1. If you're using corn on the cob, chop the corn off that cob.

2. Place a large cast-iron pan over a fire/stovetop heated to the medium. Add a drizzle of olive oil, then sauté corn, mixing, till color brightens and corn becomes crisp-tender, for almost 5 min. Put corn to a small bowl/plate.

3. In the same pan, assemble half tortilla chips. Top it with half black beans, bell pepper, diced green chilies, corn, and cheese. Add remaining chips, then top it with remaining beans, pepper, chilies, corn, and cheese. Seal loosely with aluminum foil / a lid then allow to heat 5min / till cheese is melted.

4. Take out from heat then top with salsa, sliced avocado, cilantro, sour cream, lime juice, and lettuce as desired.

2. Campfire Baked Sweet Potatoes + Chili

Prep Time: 5 min Cook Time: 30 min Serving: 4

Per serving kcal: 317

Ingredients:

- ½ tsp Salt

- 1 tbsp Chili powder

- 6 oz can Tomato paste

- 15 oz can Drained kidney beans

- 1 tbsp Olive oil

- 4 med Sweet potatoes

- 1 Diced onion

- ½ can Beer

- ½ tbsp Cumin

Directions:

1. Within embers of the campfire, cover each one of the sweet potatoes in big heavy foil & nestle them. To ensure they cook equally, flip them occasionally.

2. Get the Chili when the potatoes have been boiling. Heat the oil in the pan on med heat. Put ¾ of the minced onions till heated & sauté for a couple of mins before they begin to soften. Tomato paste, beans, beer & spices must be added. To mix, blend well. About 15 to 20 mins, boil.

3. Recover from the flame when the potatoes become tender & cooked completely. Unwrap each foil cautiously. To slice a slit into the potato, have used a knife & top it with the onions & Chili.

Notes

Equipment needed:

Chopping board + fine knife + aluminum foil + wooden spoon tongs + plates for serving

3. Grilled Blooming Onion

Prep Time: 5 min Cook Time: 30 min Serving: 3

Per serving kcal: 111

Ingredients:

- 2 tbsp Hot sauce

- 2 tbsp Chopped mozzarella cheese

- 1/2 tbsp Olive oil

- 1 large White onion

- Fresh ground pepper & salt

- 2 tbsp Chopped mild cheddar cheese

Directions:

1. Warm the grill.

2. Slice the onion between 6-8 wedges, preserving the bottom 0.5 inch small. Don't cut to bottom-leaving the bottom unchanged.

3. Cut out an aluminum foil piece.

4. Put the onion on the foil & open the onion a little slowly, pulling apart the wedges.

5. 5. Drizzle the olive oil with the onion.

6. 6. Sprinkle with pepper & salt

7. In an open onion middle, put the cheeses.

8. Drizzle the sauce over the whole onion.

9. Firmly seal it & grill it for around 30-35 mins or till the onion becomes soft.

10. Take it from the grill & open the foil smoothly.

11. Serve right away.

Notes

You can serve it as a side dish & also as an appetizer.

4. African Sweet Potato and Peanut Stew

Prep time 5 min, cook time 30 min, Serving 4

Per serving: Calories: 334kcal

Ingredients

- 2 cups Tuscan kale (destemmed n chopped)

- 1 tsp Salt

- ¼ cup Peanut butter

- 2 cups Broth

- 2 cloves (about 1 tbsp) Garlic (minced)

- 1 tbsp Oil

- 1 small Onion (diced)

- (cut into 1/4inch cubes) 1 Medium sweet potato

- 14oz can Diced tomatoes

- 2 tbsp New Mexico chili powder

- 14oz can Chickpeas (drained)

Directions

1. Heat the oil over medium heat in a Dutch oven. Add onion then sauté for almost 5 min, until the onion is translucent and starts to brown in patches. Add garlic then sauté for around 1

min until it is fragrant.

2. Add sweet potato, tomatoes, broth & their juices, chili powder, peanut butter, and salt. To guarantee that the peanut butter is fully blended in, whisk well, and there are no clumps left. Simmer, uncovered, for around 15 to 20 min / till the sweet potatoes are soft.

3. Add chickpeas and kale to Dutch oven until the sweet potatoes become soft. Once the chickpeas have been warmed, and the kale has wilted, swirl to mix, and enjoy.

5. Grilled Mexican Street Corn (Elote)

Prep Time: 5 min Cook Time: 15 min Serving: 4

Per serving kcal: 385

Ingredients:

- Chopped cilantro

- 1/2 tsp Salt

- ½ Lime juice

- 4 ears Corn

- 1/2 cup Mayo

- 1 tsp Chili powder

- 1/2 cup Crumbled Cojita

Directions:

1. After peeling your husks back, make ready the corn & cut all the silk. Replace the husks.

2. Put the corn on the campfire on the grill. Grill for 10 to 15 min, often flipping till the corn is burnt in spots and cooked through. Take it from the grill & let it cool a little so that it is secure to touch. Remove the husks and dispose of them.

3. In a shallow bowl, mix the lime juice, mayo, powder of Chili, & salt. Slather all around the corn equally. Top with the coriander & Cojita. Enjoy it.

6. Camping chilaquiles

Prep Time: 20 min Cook Time: 20 min Serving: 1

Per serving Cal: 290

Ingredients:

- Mexican crema sauce

- for 15 mins Sliced red onions & allow it to rest in rice wine vinegar

- Season with chopped fresh leaves of cilantro

- Freshly ground black pepper & salt

- ½ cup Cilantro

- 5 to 6 Eggs

- 1 16 oz can Enchilada sauce

- 1 tsp Olive oil

- 20 corn 8 pieces of tortillas

- 1 cup Roasted corn

- ½ cup Crumbled cotija cheese

- 1 Lime juice

- Toppings

- Season lime slices

- Hot sauce

Directions:

1. Dutch oven greased.

2. Open the enchilada sauce.

3. Fill the Dutch oven bottom with oil of olive. With the cheese, sauce & any seasonings, layer tortillas of corn. If needed, top with smashed eggs.

4. Please place them in a half-hour campfire. When the top is browned & cooked completely & white eggs are ready with runny yolks.

5. Season with coriander, slices of lime, & red onions pickled. If needed, eat it with hot sauce & cream. Now serve it.

7. Skillet Herb Bread

Total time: Prep: 10 min. Bake: 35 mins. **Yield:** 10 servings.

275 calories

Ingredients

- 1-1/2 cups all-purpose flour

- 2 tbsp sugar

- 4 tsp baking powder

- 1 to 1/2 tsp salt

- 1 tsp rubbed sage

- 1 tsp dried thyme

- 1 to 1/2 cups chopped celery

- 1 cup chopped onion

- 1 to 1/2 cups yellow cornmeal

- 2 ounces 1 jar drained chopped pimientos

- 3 large eggs, room temp, beaten

- 1/3 cup vegetable oil

- 1 to 1/2 cups fat-free milk

Directions

1. Combine the sugar, baking powder, flour, salt, sage and thyme in a wide dish. Combine the cornmeal, celery, pimientos and onion; blend well with the dry ingredients. Place the eggs, milk & oil in the mixture; whisk until moistened. Pour in a 10-in or 11-in greased mixture. Skillet, ovenproof. Bake for 35 to 45 mins at 400 ° or until the bread measurements are finished. Serve it warm.

8. Campfire Cheese Hash Brown Packets

Total time: Prep/Total Time: 30 mins. **Yield:** 4 servings.

329 calories

Ingredients

- 28 ounces 1 package frozen-thawed O'Brien potatoes

- 1-1/4 cups shredded divided cheddar cheese,

- 8 bacon strips, chopped & cooked

- 1/2 tsp salt

- 1/4 tsp pepper

- Large eggs hard-boiled & Pico de Gallo

Directions

1. Grill   For med-high heat or prepare a campfire. Mix 3/4 cup cheese, salt, bacon, and pepper with the potatoes.

2. Divide the mixture into 4 18x12-in   Heavy-duty bits of nonstick foil, positioning food on the dull side of the foil. Fold the foil around the potato combination, tightly covering it.

3. Place the packets over the grill or campfire. Cook each side for 6-9 mins or until the potatoes are ready. Carefully open packages to enable steam to escape, then sprinkle with any remaining cheese. Serve with eggs & Pico de Gallo if needed.

9. Campers Favorite Dip

Total time: Prep/Total Time: 15 mins. Yield: 3-1/2 cups.

250 calories

Ingredients

- 8 ounces 1 package cream cheese reduced-fat

- 15 ounces 1 can chili with beans

- 2 cups shredded cheddar cheese

- 2 sliced thinly green onions

- Tortilla chip scoops

Directions

1. Grill For med-high heat or prepare a campfire. Spread the cream cheese in the base of the 9" Disposable pie tray with foil. Place chili on top; sprinkle it with cheese.

2. Place the pan on a grill over some campfire or on some grill for 5-8 mins till the cheese is melted, then sprinkle with the green onion if needed. With chips, serve.

10. Campfire Pancakes with Peanut Maple Syrup

Total time: Prep/Total Time: 20 mins. **Yield:** 8 pancakes

407 calories

Ingredients

- 6 to 1/2 ounces 1 package, chocolate chip muffin mix

- 1 lightly beaten large egg

- 2/3 cup milk

- 1/2 cup miniature marshmallows

- 1 tbsp chunky peanut butter

- 1/4 cup butterscotch chips

- 1/4 cup maple syrup

Directions

1. Combine the muffin mix, egg & milk in a wide bowl; whisk until moistened. Fold in the chips and marshmallows.

2. Grease a griddle lightly; heat it over med heat. Pour 1/4 of a cupful of batter onto the griddle. Cook until the top bubbles are bursting, and the bottoms are golden brown. Turn over; cook until golden brown on the second side.

3. Meanwhile, until cooked thru, microwave maple syrup & peanut butter at 10-20-sec intervals. With biscuits, serve.

11. Root Beer Apple Baked Beans

Total time: Prep: 20 min. Cook: 45 mins. **Yield:** 12 servings.

255 calories

Ingredients

- 6 thickly-sliced chopped bacon strips,

- 16 ounces each 4 cans baked beans

- 21 ounces 1 can apple pie filling

- 12 ounces 1 can root beer

- 1 tsp ground ancho chili pepper

- 1 cup smoked shredded cheddar cheese

Directions

1. Using 32 to 36 charcoal briquettes/broad wood chips to prepare a med-hot campfire or grill.

2. in 10" Dutch oven, cook the bacon until crisp, over the campfire. Withdraw; remove drippings. Carry the bacon back to the pan; stir in the baked beans, root beer pie filling, and ancho chili pepper if needed.

3. cover the Dutch oven. If briquettes/wood chips are loaded with ash, place 16 to 18 briquettes on top of the Dutch oven. Place 16 to 18 briquettes on the cover of the pan.

4. Cook for 30-40 mins in order to mix the flavors. With cheese Sprinkle, the servings, if needed.

12. Eclairs on the Grill

Total time: Prep: 5 min. Grill: 5 mins, servings 6.

293 calories

Ingredients

- Stick/wooden dowel (5/8" diameter & 24 inches long)

- 3 to 1/4 ounces each 3 cups (snack-size) vanilla/chocolate pudding

- 8 ounces 1 tube seamless crescent dough sheet refrigerated

- Whipped cream

- 1/2 cup chocolate frosting

Directions

1. Grill For med-high heat or prepare a campfire. Use foil to wrap an end of a stick/wooden dowel. Unroll the crescent dough and split it into six 4" squares.   Wrap the prepared stick with one slice of dough; pinch the end & cover.

2. Grill for med-high heat or prepare a campfire or till golden brown, turning periodically. Remove from the stick until the dough is cold enough to manage. End Cooling. Repeat for the dough that remains.

3. Place the pudding in the plastic bag (resealable); in one edge, cut a tiny hole. To press the mixture in each shell, squeeze the bag. Spread it with frosting; add whipped cream to the top.

Chapter 8: Desserts

Craving for dessert can occur even during in camping. Check out the list of dessert recipes that you can make easily during camping

1. Churros Muffins

Prep time 15min, cook time 20min, Serving 24

Per serving: Calories: 89kcal

Ingredients

Muffins:

- ¼ tsp Salt
- 1 cup All-purpose flour
- ½ cup Milk
- ½ cup White sugar
- ¼ cup Butter melted
- 1 tsp Vanilla
- 1 tsp Baking powder

Churro Cinnamon Sugar Topping:

- 1 tsp Cinnamon
- ½ cup Sugar
- ¼ cup Butter

Directions

1. Preheat oven to 375 degrees F. Coat a 24 mini-muffin pan with cooking spray.

2. Mix 1/2 cup sugar and 1/4 cup butter in a large bowl. Stir in the milk and vanilla, then mix in the flour, baking powder, and salt until combined. Fill the prepared mini muffin cups about half full.

3. Bake in the preheated oven until the muffins' tops are lightly golden, 15 to 20 minutes.

4. While muffins are baking, place 1/4 cup of melted butter in a small bowl. In a separate bowl, combine 1/2 cup of sugar and cinnamon.

5. Turn the muffin tin pan over to free the muffins on the cooling rack or plate.

6. Immerse all muffins individually in the butter which is melted and roll them in the mixture of sugar-cinnamon. Let them cool and serve.

2. Banana Bread Pancakes

Prep time 5 min, cook time 25 min, Serving 16 pancakes

Per serving: Calories: 152 kcal

Ingredients

- Ghee, coconut oil, or butter for your pan

- 1 tsp Salt

- 2 tsp Cinnamon

- 2 cups Flour

- 2 Eggs

- 3 Bananas (more ripened better)

- 1½ cup Whole milk

- ¼ cup Brown sugar

- 2 tsp Baking powder

- 1 cup Chopped walnuts

Directions

At Home

1. In a sealable bag/container, add flour, cinnamon, brown sugar, baking powder, salt, and load with the remaining ingredients.

At Camp

1. In a medium bowl, place 2 bananas and mash thoroughly till smooth with a fork. Crack an egg into the mixture and add milk. Beat together the banana, the egg, and the milk till smooth.

2. Add dry ingredients to that bowl and stir with wet ingredients till well combined. Don't overmix it- small lumps are OK but some. You can add an extra 1/4 cup of milk if the batter seems too thick.

3. Over medium low - medium heat, heat non-stick pan / well-seasoned cast-iron skillet on the stove. To coat the pan, add ghee, coconut oil, or butter, then swirl. In the center of the skillet, pour ⅓cup of pancake batter and disperse some chopped walnuts on the top. Cook until the

top starts to bubble for a few minutes, and sides are set (2 to 3 min). Flip pancakes by using a spatula and cook the other side till golden.

4. For each of the pancakes, repeat with the rest of the batter, adding more ghee/oil as needed to the pan.

5. Stack the pancakes and top them with maple syrup/butter, sliced banana, and extra toasted walnuts for serving. Enjoy.

Notes

In a bag/container at home, measure and merge the flour, cinnamon, brown sugar, baking powder, and salt. Separately, pack the banana, milk, egg, and walnuts.

3. Good Snack Mix

Prep Time: 10 min Cook Time: 45 min Serving: 7

Per serving Cal: 180

Ingredients:

- 1 to ½ cups Salted cashews

- 2 cups Crispix

- 1/2 tsp Garlic powder

- 1 tbsp Canola oil

- 3 tbsp Melted butter

- 4 tsp Worcestershire sauce

- 1 tsp Seasoned salt

- 2 cups Corn Chex

- 2 cups Shredded wheat bite-sized

Directions:

1. Oven preheated to 250 degrees. The first five ingredients are mixed, toss

   with cashews & cereals, then cover equally. Spread into the skillet coated with the cooking spray.

2. Cook for forty-five mins, mixing every fifteen minutes. Cool perfectly before saving it in the airtight jar.

4. S' mores (dessert)

Prep Time: 15 min Serving: 4

Per serving Cal: 271

Ingredients:

- 4 large Marshmallows

- 4 whole Halved graham crackers

- 4 Cookies of Oreo

- 3 tbsp Peanut butter creamy

- 1 Chocolate milk candy bar

Directions:

1. Spread butter peanut on all sides of every Oreo cookie; put half of each on a graham cracker. Garnish with chocolate.

2. Toast the marshmallows six in by using a big metal skewer from med-high heat till its color changes to a golden brown, turning often. Put on the chocolate, cover with the graham crackers leftover. Serve right away.

5. Red wine hot chocolate recipe

Prep Time: 5 min Cook Time: 5 min Serving: 1

Per serving Cal: 363

Ingredients:

- Pinch of salt

- 1/2 tsp Cinnamon

- 2 tbsp Cocoa powder

- Cocoa Mugs

- Boiling pan

- Mixing spoon

- 2 cup Red wine

- 2 tbsp Sugar

- 4 cup Milk

Directions:

In a broad saucepan, mix the sugar, cinnamon & cocoa powder. Place the red wine & milk then boil on med heat for around five min, often stirring, till warm & smooth.

Enjoy it.

6. Campfire Banana Boats

Prep Time: 5 min Cook Time: 10 min Serving: 1

Per serving kcal: 179

Ingredients:

Classic banana boat

- 1 graham Cracker square
- 2 tbsp Milk chocolate
- Banana 1
- 8 mini Marshmallows

Directions:

1. Take the banana & slice it down the center (along the concave edge) with the skin already. Not even all the way through, however, till the tip of the knife grazes the skin. Tear slightly apart from the peel & banana.

2. Into the middle of the banana put the tiny marshmallows & chocolate

3. Cover the banana in foil. Please put it on a campfire or barbecue for around 10 minutes before the fillings have melted, and the banana has cooked.

4. Unwrap the banana & season it with a smashed graham cracker.

Notes

Creative boat fillings of banana

Raspberry hazelnuts: raspberries + Nutella + minced hazelnuts + banana

Vegan: dark chocolate + dandies' tiny marshmallows + banana

Samoas: chocolate morsels + sauce of caramel + banana + toasted coconut

Honey ginger: honey + banana + dark/white chocolate + candied ginger

Split of banana: chocolate milk + banana + cherries + marshmallows

7. Energy-Boosting Trail Mix

Prep Time: 10 min Cook Time: 35 minutes kcal: 218

Ingredients:

- ¾ cup Chocolate chips dark

- ½ cup Seeds of raw sunflower

- 1 cup raw walnuts

- 1 cup Unsweetened flakes of coconut

- 1 cup Raw almonds

- 1 cup Cashews

- 1 cup Dried cherries/cranberries

Directions

1. Put the coconut flakes on the stove in a shallow skillet. Toast on med-low flame,

   till its color changes to lightly golden & fragrant, nicely mixing occasionally. It should just take 2 to 3 mins to do this; closely see the coconut so it may not burn. Allow it to cool before combining it with some other ingredients.

2. In a wide bowl/ storage jar, put the toasted coconut & all the rest of the ingredients; mix it. Place the trail mix at an enclosed jar at room temp or split it into zip-top baggies into separate pieces.

Chapter 9: Sandwiches or Snacks

1. Camping breakfast sandwich

Prep Time: 5 min Cook Time: 20 min Serving: 1

Ingredients:

- Butter

- 4 Eggs

- 4 English muffins bay's sourdough

- 2 cups Remaining BBQ pulled pork

- 4 slices Cheddar cheese

Directions:

1. Crisp the English muffins with a little butter in a med cast iron skillet till crispy & golden.

2. In a pan, heat the remaining pork & set it aside.

3. Fry the eggs.

Fill ½ cup of pulled pork, a piece of cheddar cheese & a runny egg with the English muffin. Cover in foil & put over the heat till the cheese is melted

2. Grilled Caprese Sandwich

Prep Time: 5 min Cook Time: 10 min Serving: 2

Per serving kcal: 667

Ingredients:

- Pepper & salt

- 4 oz Sliced into rounds mozzarclla cheese

- 1 tbsp Oil

- 2 to 3 Ripe tomatoes

- 2 6-inch Sliced in half lengthwise baguettes

- 1/3 cup Prepared pesto

Directions:

1. Into the thick circles, cut the tomatoes & rub with oil. Please put it on the grill and cook till blackened in spots & warmed fully, cook five mins each side. If necessary, grill/barbecue the cut baguettes sides.

2. Spread pesto on the baguettes, cut sides for assembly, then layer the onions, cheese, & basil if included. Season with pepper and salt. Now enjoy it.

3. Easy no-knead skillet bread

Prep Time: 1hr 45 min Cook Time: 35 min per serving Cal: 98

Ingredients:

- 3 tbsp Olive oil about
- 1/2 tbsp Kosher salt
- 4 1/3 cups Bread flour
- 1 package Rapid rise yeast
- 2 cups Warm water

Directions:

1. Mix all the yeast, salt & flour in a big mixing bowl. You may also add your preference of spices/herbs here.

2. In the bowl, put warm water. Be sure that the water is not hot & just warm. Stir till well mixed, with a rubber spatula/spoon. It's going to be a sticky dough, approximately like a dense batter.

3. Cover with aluminum foil/towel & let stay till around double in size at room temp. This would take around 45 min for fast rise yeast and active dry yeast, an hour & a half.

4. Don't punch this dough down onto the bottom in a cast iron pan or some similar oven protected skillet put around 1 tablespoon of oil.

5. Drizzle the dough with about a tablespoon of oil and drizzle it on your side, too. Clean the hands with the grease, which will allow the dough not to adhere. Strip the dough from the sides of the bowl carefully and then catch everything in your hands. Form it softly into a disc. Since the dough is sticky, this will be sort of complicated, but please try your utmost. It needn't have to be fine.

6. In the oiled skillet, put the dough and cover it loosely with a towel. Let the yeast grow again until it is full of air-about 30 minutes for quick growing yeast and 1 hour for active dry yeast.

7. Oven preheated to 205° c

8. Drizzle the top of the bread with more oil, then outline the dough with such a knife to make the x or a few slices around the top. If needed, toss with rosemary leaves & coarse salt.

9. Bake till the top begins to brown, for around 35 to 40 mins. After this, switch the broiler on for around five min & keep an eye on the bread.

10. Let the bread to chill for one hour &, ideally, longer before slicing. Before slicing, having the bread cool would solidify its texture & make it remain fresh longer, too.

11. Keep sliced bread exposed on a chopping board for around 2 days at room temperature, split side down. Then put it into the bag as well as seal it. After 2 days, slice this up & freeze. This refreshes well in the toaster after being frozen.

4. Sausage Egg & Cheese Breakfast Sandwiches with Sriracha Honey Sauce

Prep Time: 5 min Cook Time: 10 min Serving: 6

Per serving kcal: 600

Ingredients:

- 1 tsp Salt

- 1-pound Ground pork

- Sausage patties

- 2 tsp Dried herbs

    Sriracha honey sauce

- 2 tbsp Sriracha

- 1/2 cup Honey

Sandwich assembly

- 6 English muffins

- 6 Eggs

- 6 Cheese slices

Directions:

1. Prepare the sausages: in a wide bowl, combine spices, the ground pork & salt till completely mixed. Shape into six patties of equal size, thinking that they would also shrink a little while cooking.

2. Prepare the sauce: in a tiny bowl, add the honey & sriracha together and mix it. Just set aside.

3. Cook: on over the stovetop/campfire, warm a skillet/griddle. Put the sausages on the surface once heated, & cook till browned, 2 to 3 min. Turn & cook till browned on the other hand, for another 2 to 3 mins. Besides that, as needed, boil the eggs & toast some muffins.

4. Assemble & serve: spread the honey sriracha sauce on muffins after this layer with the egg, cheese slice & sausage patty. Serve now.

Notes

Made the patties of sausage and put them in your cooler inside an air-tight jar. The day you prepare your meal in the morning begins with phase 2.

By swapping the patties of sausage with the vegetarian substitute, this recipe may be turned vegetarian.

5. Cheesy Asparagus One Pot Orzo

Prep time 5 min, cook time 10 min, Serving 2

Per serving kcal: 523

Ingredients

- 2 tbsp Pine nuts

- 1/2 cup Shredded cheese

- 1/2 tsp Salt

- 1/2 tsp Dried basil

- 1/2 tbsp Olive Oil

- 2 cups Water

- 1/2 lb. Asparagus

- 1 cup Orzo

- 1/2 tsp Dried thyme

- 1/2 tsp Garlic powder

- 1/4 tsp Red pepper flakes

- 1/4 cup Tomatoes (sun-dried + chopped)

Directions

1. Cut off then Discard hard ends of the asparagus, and then slice the asparagus into 1" bits.

2. In a pot, add asparagus, orzo, water, oil, and all the spices. Bring to the low boil and cook till the orzo is soft (for an additional 5 min).

3. Add cheese, pine nuts, and sun-dried tomatoes after reducing the heat. Stir till you've melted the cheese.

4. Remove from the heat, season with pepper and salt to taste, and enjoy.

6. Camp Stove Chilaquiles

Prep time 5 min, cook time 20 min, Serving 2

Per serving: Calories: 550 kcal

Ingredients

- 2 to 4 Eggs

- 1 -7 oz can El Pato

- ½ Red onion (diced),

- 6 Corn tortillas (chopped into wedges),

- ⅓ cup Vegetable oil

- 2 cloves Garlic (minced),

- ½ tsp Salt

Directions

1. Heat the oil over high heat in a pan. Add tortilla triangles in such a single layer once the oil becomes hot, then fry for a couple of mins till golden brown, flipping once. Remove and put aside to drain (on paper towel). With the rest of the tortillas, repeat.

2. Decrease the heat to medium. Add red onions to remaining oil and saute for a couple of mins before they start to soften. Add garlic and saute for around 30 seconds, then add to the skillet the salt, tomato sauce, and water splash. Simmer, and add fried tortillas. To coat, stir.

3. Shift the tortillas to the skillet's outer edges to cook eggs to build a well in the center. Drop eggs into the sauce to cook them to your taste. You can scramble/cover the pan to enable them to easily poach in sauce.

4. With toppings of your choosing, serve.

Notes

You could do this phase at home and pack them with you if you would not want to deal with the frying of tortillas at camp / you can choose market bought tortilla - no criticism from us.

7. Wyoming Cowboy Cookies

Total time: Prep: 25 min. Bake: 15 mins. **Yield:** 6 dozen.

211 calories

Ingredients

- 1 c shredded sweetened coconut

- 1 c softened butter

- 3/4 c pecans (chopped)

- 1-1/2 c brown sugar (packed)

- 2 eggs, room temp

- 1/2 c sugar

- 1-1/2 tsp vanilla extract

- 2 c all-purpose flour

- 1 tsp baking soda

- 1/2 tsp salt

- 12 ounces 2 c chocolate chips

- 2 c oats

Directions

1. Place on a 15x10x1" coconut & pecans. baking pan. Bake for 6- 8 mins at 350 ° until its toasted, stirring after 2 minutes. Set to cool aside.

2. Crème butter & sugar in a big bowl until fluffy and light. Mix in the vanilla and eggs; blend well. Mix the baking soda, flour and salt; Add to the creamed mixture and beat well. Add the chocolate chips, oats, toasted coconut then pecans, then combine well.

3. Drop onto oiled baking sheets with rounded teaspoonfuls. Bake for 12 mins or till browned at 350 °. to cool Remove to wire shelves.

8. Cherry-Chocolate Pudgy Pie

Total time: Prep/Total Time: 10 mins. **Yield:** 1 serving.

309 calories

Ingredients

- 2 slices white bread

- 1 tbsp chopped almonds

- 3 tbsp cherry pie filling

- 1 tbsp semisweet chocolate chips

Directions

1. Use an oiled sandwich iron to put 1 slice of bread. Spread with pie filling; finish with chocolate chips, almonds and leftover slices of bread.

2. Cook until golden brown & heated through, 3 to 6 minutes, rotating periodically over the hot campfire.

9. Fruit & Almond Bites

Total time: Prep: 40 min. + chilling, **Yield:** about 4 dozen.

86 calories

Ingredients

- 3-3/4 cups almonds sliced, divided
- 1/4 tsp almond extract
- 1/4 cup honey
- 2 cups dried apricots finely chopped
- 1 cup dried cherries/cranberries finely chopped
- 1 cup pistachios, toasted finely chopped

Directions

1. In a food processor, add 1-1/4 cups of almonds; pulse till finely chopped. In a shallow dish, remove the almonds; retain to coat.

2. To the food processor, add the leftover 2-1/2 cups of almonds; pulse until thinly sliced. Add extract. Add honey gradually while processing. Stir in the apricots & cherries in a bowl. Divide the mixture into six parts; mold each one into a 1/2"-thick roll. Wrap it in plastic then refrigerate for around 1 hour till firm.

3. Unwrap the rolls and split them into 1-1/2-" bits. Roll half of the bits into reserved almonds, gently pressing them to stay together. Roll out half the available pistachios. Individually wrap it in the wax paper if needed, twist end to close. Place in airtight packages, if unwrapped, within waxed paper layers.

10. Campfire Cinnamon Twists

Total time: Prep/Total Time: 25 mins. Servings 16.

98 calories

Ingredients

- 2 tsp ground cinnamon

- 1/4 cup sugar

- 12.4 ounces 1 tube refrigerated cinnamon rolls

- 2 tbsp butter, melted

Directions

1. Combine the cinnamon and sugar. Remove the icing from the cinnamon rolls; move for drizzling to some resealable plastic bag.

2. Separate rolls; split in half, each one. Roll into 6" ropes. Wrap each rope firmly, starting at 1/2 in, around a large steel skewer

3. Cook over some hot campfire for around 5 mins, turning periodically, till golden brown. Brush it with butter then sprinkle with blended sugar. Cut 1 corner of the icing bag then drizzle the icing over the twists.

11. Bratwurst Supper

Total time: Prep: 10 min. Grill: 45 mins. Servings 12.

524 calories

Ingredients

- 3 lbs. uncooked bratwurst links
- 3 lbs. small red potatoes, in wedges form
- 1 lb. baby carrots
- 1 red onion, sliced & separated in rings

- 4-1/2 ounces each 2 jars whole mushrooms, drained

- 1/4 cup cubed butter

- 1 onion soup mix

- 2 tbsp soy sauce

- 1/2 tsp pepper

Directions

1. Arrange a heavy-duty foil double thickness (about 17x15") on the flat surface on each of the 2 foil packages.

2. Split the brats into thirds. Divide equally between the 2 Dbl-layer foil rectangles, the brats, carrots, potatoes, onion and mushrooms. Dots it with butter. With soup blend, pepper and soy sauce Sprinkle it. Bring together the ends of the foil; crimp together to seal, making 2 wide packages. Tightly seal

3. Grill, wrapped, for 23-28 mins on either side over med heat or until the vegetables are soft and no longer pink is the sausage. To allow the steam to escape, open the foil carefully.

12. Campfire Bundles

Total time: Prep: 15 min. Grill: 1 hour, **servings** 6.

582 calories

Ingredients

- 1 sweet onion, sliced

- 1 green pepper

- 1 sweet red pepper

- 1 sweet yellow pepper

- 4 med potatoes, cut in 1/4" slices

- 1 head cabbage, sliced

- 6 med carrots, cut into ¼" slices

- 2 med tomatoes, chopped

- 1/2 cup cubed butter

- 1 - 1-1/2 lbs. smoked Polish sausage, cut in ½" slices

- 1 tsp salt

- 1/2 tsp pepper

Directions

1. Put vegetables (about 18". square) on 3 dual thicknesses of heavy-duty foil. Top with sausage, then sprinkle with sugar. Using salt & pepper to sprinkle. Fold the foil over each mixture; tightly seal it.

2. Grill, sealed, for 30 minutes over med heat. Turn and grill for about 30 mins more till the vegetables are soft. To allow the steam to escape, open the foil carefully.

Chapter 10: Low Carb Recipes

Some people prefer take diet with low carb. So, this chapter is about all such low carb recipes that people can easily make to fulfil their appetite

1. Low-carb raspberry cheesecake swirl brownies

Prep time 15 min, cook time 40 min, Serving 24

Per serving kcal: 171

Ingredients

Brownie batter

- ¼ tsp Salt

- 1 cup Almond flour

- Erythritol 1 cup

- 4 oz., chopped Baking chocolate sugar-free

- 6 oz. Butter

- 4 large Eggs

- 2 tsp Vanilla extract

Cream cheese filling

- 6 oz Fresh raspberries

- 1 tsp (optional) Raspberry extract

- 1 large Egg

- 10 oz., softened Cream cheese

- 1/3 cup Powdered erythritol

- 2 tsp Vanilla extract

- 1 tbsp Lemon juice

Directions

1. At first, Preheat the oven to 175 ° C (350 ° F).

2. Line a baking dish of 9", x13" (20x30 cm) with the parchment paper so that the edges come over the dish and can be utilized to lift the brownies (baked) from the pan easily.

3. Melt the butter and chocolate on low heat in a small saucepan OR microwave. When it's melted, add sweetener, and stir till the sweetener is fully dissolved

4. Mix the eggs, vanilla extract, almond flour, and salt in a large bowl. Add the mixture of melted chocolate when thoroughly mixed and stir to combine. In the prepared pan, slowly pour the mixture into it.

5. Mix the powdered sweetener and cream cheese using a stand mixer or a hand mixer. Add the egg when it's creamy n smooth and mix well.

6. Whisk in the vanilla extract, lemon juice, and raspberry extract.

7. Fold in the new raspberries (but softly).

8. Over brownie batter, drop big spoonsfuls of the mixture of cheesecake. Swirl the Cheesecake Batter into the Brownie Batter with a knife by drawing the tip horizontally and vertically through the batter.

9. Bake until finished, from (30 - 40 min). You shouldn't overbake. Until serving, let it cools completely.

Notes

Refrigerate the leftovers.

2. Keto rhubarb tart

Prep time 15 min, cook time 45 min, Serving 8

Per serving kcal: 515

Ingredients

Crust

- 3 oz. Butter

- 1/3 cup Erythritol

- 6 oz. Almond flour

- 3/4 oz Coconut (Unsweetened and finely shredded),

Almond cream filling

- 7 oz. Rhubarb

- 3 Eggs

- 1/2 cup Erythritol

- 4 1/4 oz. Butter (softened)

- 1 3/4 cups Almond flour

- 1 tsp Vanilla extract

Directions

1. Preheat the stove to 180 ° C (360 ° F). Grease the 9-inch (24cm) tart pan gently.

2. In a mixing bowl, put almond flour, shredded coconut, and erythritol, and whisk to blend.

3. In a microwave-safe container, melt the butter and add in the dry ingredients. Blend well till a loose dough is made.

4. Use a spoon thinly across the sides and in the middle of your tart pan to spoon the dough, and then push tightly with your fingertips into place. Place the crust in the oven and cook it for 10 min.

5. Place the melted butter along with erythritol in the bowl of a mixer (when the crust is being baked) and beat till pale and fluffy. In batches, add almond flour, Eggs, and Vanilla, mixing well in b/w additions.

6. Take the tart crust out of the oven and keep the oven going.

7. Peel the long strips from the rhubarb stalks using the vegetable peeler and place them on one side.

8. Spoon filling into the tart shell, spiral the rhubarb's strips and drive them into the filling tightly. Feel free doing some loose spirals, for variety, and some rigid ones.

9. Bake for 35 more min.

Notes

To finish the crust's ends, use a 1/4 cup scale. To have a lovely sharp return, press it tightly against the seam of a crust.

Store the tart, well-sealed, for up to five days in a refrigerator. Please remember that they can weaken the crust.

3. Whipped dairy-free low-carb (Dalgona) coffee

Prep time 5 min, cook time 0 min, Serving 2

Per serving kcal: 40

Ingredients

- ½ cup Ice cubes

- 1 tsp Optional: vanilla extract

- 1½ tbsp Erythritol

- 1½ tbsp (Instant coffee powder) Espresso,

- 2 tbsp Hot / Boiled water

- 1½ cups Unsweetened Almond Milk / Coconut Milk

Directions

1. Using either a whisk, hand-held frother, or an immersion blender for the whipped topping (using the first two ways, whipping time would be significantly longer).

2. In a pint-sized glass jar or narrow glass, whisk together the erythritol, Espresso Powder, and warm water.

3. Insert immersion blender into a glass and whisk for about 3 min at a high pace. When the dark coffee mixture is whipped, it rises in thickness and makes a whipped cream that is light-colored.

4. Fill up the large glass, around 2/3 full, with ice. Pour in the vanilla extract, almond milk, and blend.

5. Spoon the whipped coffee on top, then just before eating, whisk together.

Notes

Almond Milk can be replaced by coconut milk, or you can use them both. You should also use full-fat milk/cream combined with water instead of almond milk when you use dairy goods. Any instant coffee would work, but espresso is a little stronger and gives a more concentrated flavor.

To keep the whip more stable, we can use a granulated sweetener. Without sweetener, it would not whip properly.

4. Keto chopped hoagie bowl

Prep time 15 min Cook time 0 min, Serving 8

Per serving kcal: 421

Ingredients

Bowl

- ¼ Red onion (finely diced)
- 7oz Cucumber (peeled n chopped)
- 3 ½ oz Lettuce (shredded)
- 8 oz Smoked deli ham, chopped
- 8oz Roasted Turkey (chopped)
- 8oz Genoa Salami (chopped)
- 4oz Mild cheddar cheese (chopped)
- 5 1/3 oz Grape tomatoes
- 3oz Pickled Banana Peppers (chopped rings)

Sauce

- ½ tsp Dried oregano
- 1 tsp Dried basil
- 2 tbsp Olive Oil
- ¾ cup Mayonnaise
- ¼ cup Red wine vinegar
- ½ tsp Italian seasoning

Directions

1. Put all the ingredients for the bowl in a big serving bowl then set aside.

2. Mix all the ingredients for the sauce in a separate bowl.

3. Over the meat, cheese, and veggies, pour the sauce and stir/toss to combine.

Notes

In this recipe, use grape tomatoes instead of chopped tomatoes to keep it for longer, and for those that don't enjoy tomatoes can simply ignore them.

You may also wait till just before serve to incorporate the lettuce so that it remains crisp.

You can miss the tomatoes entirely if you want to reduce the carb count, but don't miss the cucumbers, peppers, or the red onions.

5. Salad in a jar

Prep time 10 min, cook time 0 min, Serving 1

Per serving kcal: 875

Ingredients

- ¼ cup Mayonnaise or Olive Oil

- 1oz. Cherry Tomatoes

- 1 Avocado

- ½ Scallion, sliced

- 1 oz. Leafy greens

- 1 Carrot

- 1oz.Red Bell peppers

- 4oz Smoked salmon/rotisserie chicken

Directions

1. Shred the veggies or chop them.

2. Next, at the bottom of the jar, place dark leafy greens.

3. Add in layers of scallion, avocado, carrot, bell peppers, and tomato.

4. Top the Smoked salmon/Grilled chicken

5. Just before serving, add mayo.

Notes

We've chosen to top the salad with smoked salmon and grilled chicken, but you can use your own favorite protein, mackerel, boiled eggs, canned tuna, or any other kind of cold cuts of your choice, of course. Great flavorful additions include olives, seeds, nuts, and cheese cubes.

6. Keto pierogis filled with bacon and mushroom

Prep time 15 min Cook time 20 min, Serving 4

Per serving kcal: 861

Ingredients

Filling

- ¼ tsp Pepper
- 5oz. Cream cheese.
- 2oz. Fresh spinach
- 3oz. Mushrooms
- 2 cloves Garlic (finely chopped),
- 2 tsp Butter
- 1 Shallot (finely chopped)
- 5oz. Bacon
- 2oz Parmesan cheese (grated),
- ½ tsp Salt

Pierogi dough

- 1 beaten Egg (to brush the top of pierogi),
- 3oz Butter
- 1 tsp Baking powder
- 6oz Shredded cheese
- ½ tsp Salt
- ¼ cup Coconut flour
- ½ cup Almond flour

- 1 Egg

Directions

1. Begin with filling. Sauté the butter with shallots, cloves, bacon, mushrooms, and spinach till they turn a good color: pepper and salt.

2. Turn the heat down then add parmesan cheese and cream cheese. Stir and simmer for one more min. Set aside, then let cool off.

3. Preheat oven to 175 ° C (350 ° F). In a bowl, combine all the dried ingredients.

4. In a skillet (on low heat), melt the cheese and butter together. For the smooth batter, whisk thoroughly. Turn off the heat.

5. In the mixture, add the egg and keep mixing. The dry ingredients are applied and mixed into a strong dough.

6. Separate the dough into 4 balls and flatten them (using a rolling pin) into four round pieces, around ⅕inch (½cm) thin and 7 inches (18cm) in the diameter.

7. Add filling in a generous amount, on every piece of dough (only on 1 half of every piece)

8. Fold, then cover the sides using your fingers/fork.

9. Bake for 20min (after brushing with the beaten egg), till the pierogis, become gold. Serve with

dressing and a salad.

Notes

Pierogis may be kept in the freezer.

7. Keto avocado pie

Prep time 25 min, cook time 40 min, Serving 4

Per serving kcal: 1119

Ingredients

Pie crust

- ¼ cup Water

- 3 tbsp olive oil / Coconut Oil

- 1 tsp Psyllium Husk (Ground) powder

- ¼ cup Sesame seeds

- ¾ cup Almond flour

- ¼ cup Coconut flour

- 1 tsp Baking powder

- 1 pinch Salt

- 1 Egg

Filling

- 4oz. cream cheese

- ½ tsp Onion powder

- 1 cup Mayonnaise

- 2 Ripe avocados

- 2 tablespoons Fresh cilantro (nicely chopped),

- 5oz Shredded cheese

- 1 Red chili pepper (nicely chopped)

- 3 Eggs
- ¼ tsp Salt

Directions

1. Preheat your oven to 175 ° C (350 ° F). For a few minutes, combine all the ingredients for pie dough in the food processor till the dough forms a sphere. If you do not own a food processor, only use either a fork or your hands for kneading those ingredients together in the bowl.

2. Attach the parchment paper piece to the springform skillet, not larger than 12inch (26cm) in diameter. When it's finished, the springform pan makes the pie simpler to lift. Grease the skillet.

3. Spread the dough into the skillet. Use the fingertips or oiled spatula. For 10 to 15 min, pre-bake the crust.

4. Cut the avocado into two. Remove the pit, peel, and dice. Remove seeds from the chili and chop nicely. In a bowl, put the avocado and chili and then blend with other ingredients.

5. Pour the mixture into the pie crust. Bake till softly golden brown / 35 min. For a few mins, let cool and serve with a green salad.

Notes

This pie is as tasty as freshly cooked the next day. In the fridge, it even holds well. So, just put a slice into your lunch box for a super-satisfying meal. Or load your favorite basket with a few slices and go out for a summer picnic. Or for a quick weeknight meal, reheat a few bits.

8. BLTA lettuce wraps

Prep time 15 min, cook time 5 min, Serving 2

Per serving: Net carbs: 4 g, Fat: 56 g, Protein: 13 g, kcal: 586

Ingredients

- Pepper and Salt

- Avocado half

- 3 tbsp Mayonnaise

- 6oz Bacon (cut in slices)

- 2oz Lettuce (2 leaves per serving)

- 1 Tomato (cut in slices)

Directions

1. Fry the bacon till crispy (around 5 min), in a wide skillet over medium heat. To cool, set aside on the paper towel-lined tray. Cut each strip into half crosswise when cold enough to treat.

2. On each of the lettuce leaves, squeeze 1 line of mayo. Put a half-slice of tomato, 3 and a half

3. slice of bacon, and one slice of avocado on top of each vine. Season with pepper and salt to taste and enjoy it.

9. Gluten-free wrap with tuna and egg

Prep time 15 min Cook time 15 min, Serving 4

Per serving kcal: 726

Ingredients

- 1 tsp Psyllium husk (Ground) powder

- Salt ½ teaspoon

- 1 tbsp Dried parsley

- 1 Egg white

- 6oz. Shredded Cheese

- ½ lb. Cauliflower

- 1 Egg

- 2 tbsp Light Olive Oil

- ½ tsp Optional: ground cumin

- ¼ tsp Ground black pepper

Serving

- Salt n Ground black pepper

- 7oz. Kohlrabi's

- 10oz Tuna in Olive Oil

- ½ tsp Chili flakes

- 1 tbsp Wasabis paste

- ½ cup Mayonnaise

- ½ lb. Cottage cheese

- 4 Eggs

- 2oz. Pea Sprouts

Directions

Wraps

1. Preheat oven to 175 ° C (350 ° F). Split the cauliflower into smaller bits and pulse it into crumbs in the food processor.

2. Apply the rest wrap ingredients and combine them to form a smooth batter. Let it rests for 5-10 min.

3. Spread that batter, about 1/4"(5mm) deep, on the Baking Sheet lined with the parchment paper.

4. Bake for 15 min (in the oven) before it turns a pleasant golden color. Remove it from the oven and transfer the bread onto another Parchment Paper (sheet), directly upside down.

5. Return to the oven then bakes for a couple more min. Detach from the oven then break into separate parts. Let it cool.

Filling

1. For 8 min, put eggs in the boiling water.

2. Combine the mayonnaise, cottage cheese, chili, and wasabi paste. Season it with pepper and salt.

3. With a sharp knife / coarse grater, thinly slice/shred the kohlrabi. Scatter the fillings on wraps. Now Fold together

Notes

The 2nd best part about the wraps is that you can modify both wrap and filling according to your own specific tastes. So be imaginative and each time you serve them, assemble a new mix.

10. Keto salmon pie

Prep time 15 min, cook time 40 min, Serving 4

Per serving kcal: 1045

Ingredients

Pie crust

- ¾ cup Almond flour

- 4 tbsp Sesame seeds

- 4 tbsp Coconut flour

- 1 tbsp Psyllium husk (ground) powder

- 1 tsp Baking powder

- Salt

- 3 tbsp Olive Oil / Coconut Oil

- 1 Egg

- 4 tbsp Water

Filling

- 8oz. Smoked salmon

- 1 cup Mayonnaise

- 2 tbsp Fresh dill (chopped finely)

- 3 Eggs

- ½ tsp Onion powder

- ¼ tsp Ground black pepper

- 5 oz. Shredded cheese

- 5 oz. Cream cheese

Directions

1. Preheat your oven to 175 ° C (350 ° F).

2. In a food processor equipped with a Plastic Pastry blade, put Pie Dough ingredients in. Pulse till the mixture becomes a ball. You should use a fork to mix that dough if you do not own a food processor.

3. In a 10-inch (23cm) springform skillet, fit in a piece of parchment paper.

4. Oil your fingertips / a spatula, then press that dough into the spring pan gently. For 10-15 min, Prebake the crust / till finely browned.

5. Combine all the filling ingredients, except for the salmon, and pour them onto the pie crust. Add salmon and bake till the pie is golden brown / 35 min.

6. Leave to cool for a few mins and serve with salad other veggies.

Notes

Feel free to exchange cured, grilled salmon OR boiled in for smoked salmon. Only make sure the salt and spices are balanced appropriately. And don't be scared to have things done ahead of time. This pie freezes well, so for a quick midweek meal, you can keep one on hand.

Conclusion

Camping is an adventurous and essential outdoor ritual for many, a dreamlike natural phenomenon that has served as the centerpiece of backwoods gatherings for centuries. Your relaxation and desire to love your trip to the fullest degree will significantly influence how you prepare for camping and what kind of recipes you follow to make your trip even more memorable. Hence this is a comprehensive guide for camp survival and healthy food. We hope this book could be a real friend to you and encourage you to come up with your very own inventive modifications.

Printed in Great Britain
by Amazon

53562228R00095